MW00974605

the series .... reform

Patricia A. Wasley	Ann Lieberman	Joseph P. McDonald
University	Senior Scholar,	New York
of Washington	Stanford University	University

SERIES EDITORS

(Continued)

the series on school reform, *continued*

How Teachers Become Leaders

LEARNING FROM PRACTICE AND RESEARCH

Ann Lieberman
Linda D. Friedrich

Teachers College
Columbia University
New York and London

Published by Teachers College Press, 1234 Amsterdam Avenue, New York, NY 10027

The vignettes in this book are reprinted with permission from the National Writing Project (NWP). The mission of NWP is to focus the knowledge, expertise, and leadership of our nation's educators on sustained efforts to improve writing and learning for all learners.

"First Reader" from *Questions About Angels*, by Billy Collins, © 1991. Reprinted by permission of the University of Pittsburgh Press.

Library of Congress Cataloging-in-Publication Data

How teachers become leaders : learning from practice and research / Ann Lieberman, Linda D. Friedrich, [editors].
     p. cm. — (series on school reform)
  Includes bibliographical references and index.
  ISBN 978-0-8077-5128-2 (pbk. : alk. paper)
    1. Teaching—Research.   2. Teacher participation in administration.   3. Teachers—In-service training.   4. Educational leadership.   I. Lieberman, Ann.   II. Friedrich, Linda.
  LB1028.H638 2010
  371.1'06—dc22

                                       2010021552

ISBN 978-0-8077-5128-2 (paperback)

Printed on acid-free paper
Manufactured in the United States of America

17 16 15 14 13 12 11 10   8 7 6 5 4 3 2 1

Contents

Acknowledgments

As colleagues, we approached the writing of this book with great excitement. We wanted teachers who were working in leadership positions to teach us and the field how they learned to lead. And we hoped to use their writing and their words to show their experiences. Any collaboration involving so many people reads like the credits of a movie.

First and foremost are the 31 teacher-leaders who wrote, revised, and wrote again about their learning of leadership. They come from all over the United States and play many leadership roles in their schools, districts, states, and National Writing Project sites. We acknowledge: Anne H. Aliverti, Denise Amos, Benjamin Bates, Carrie Brennan, Cec Carmack, Astra Cherry, Elizabeth A. Davis, Dina Sechio DeCristofaro, Lynne R. Dorfman, Mimi Dyer, Paul Epstein, Deidré R. Farmbry, Anna Gilgoff, Shayne Goodrum, C. Lynn Jacobs, Christy James, Kim Larson, Yarda Leflet, Ronni Tobman Michelen, Nancy King Mildrum, Kathleen O'Shaughnessy, Scott Peterson, Gretchen Kuhn Phillips, Meredith Pike-Baky, Austen Reilley, Amy Schrader, Karen Smith, Linda Tatman, Kristen Turner, Carrie Usui, and Lucy Ware.

During the first half of 2006, six of us worked with smaller groups of these teacher-leaders to facilitate writing response groups and to serve as sounding boards during and between our two writing retreats. Liza Percer collaborated closely with us to design the early phases of the project, facilitate a writing group, and work with one-third of the writers between writing retreats. Ralph Cordova, Janis Cramer, and Sylvia Spruill each facilitated response groups at the retreats. We want to thank all of them for working with us so that the teacher-leaders felt that their writing reflected their perspectives about their leadership.

We would like to acknowledge the National Writing Project for sponsoring this research project and for encouraging us to do it right and do it well. We want to give a special thanks to Sharon Washington, Judy Buchanan, and Paul LeMahieu, all of the National Writing Project, for their close reading of our manuscript and helping us refine and clarify the complexities of our work. We also thank Judith Bess for sharpening our prose.

Behind every project there are many people who helped in small and large ways. We appreciate the assistance we have received analyzing the survey data from Sela Fessehaie and Ayumi Nagase and the focus group interview data from Sarah Hall. We would like to thank the many staff members at the National Writing Project who have addressed the countless details involved in this project: Rebecca C. Brown, Diana Lee, Natalie Pham-Gia, Rachel Pringle, and Carisa Lubeck.

Last, but not least we wish to thank our significant others Ernie and Gail for supporting us through this complicated, collaborative project.

—Ann Lieberman and Linda Friedrich

Introduction

Over the past 3 decades, policy makers, researchers, and educators have given renewed attention to the roles that leaders play in creating powerful learning environments for students. They view leadership as emerging at all levels of the system, from classrooms to state departments of education. Leaders, whether playing formal or informal roles, need to exhibit both broad and deep knowledge. In particular, policy makers and researchers now call for teachers to step into leadership because of their intimate knowledge of students, subject matter, and teaching. Although numerous articles and books advocate for teacher leadership (Lieberman & Miller, 2004; Mangin & Stoelinga, 2008; Spillane & Diamond, 2007; York-Barr & Duke, 2004), few, if any, focus on *how* teachers *learn* to lead in their own words. Thus, in this book, we ask and answer the following questions:

- How do teachers learn to lead?
- What does this learning look like in practice?
- What problems do teacher-leaders face and how do they learn from them? and
- How does teachers' leadership differ from popular ideas about leadership?

OUR PROJECT: LEARNING HOW TEACHERS BECOME LEADERS

To answer our questions, we invited 31 educators who have participated in the National Writing Project to write vignettes (Lieberman, 1987; Miles, 1990) about a slice of their leadership experience, with an emphasis on their learning. Previous studies suggest that this form of data collection helps individuals show the variety of activities, strategies, and tactics that they use over time (Miles, Saxl, & Lieberman, 1988). When a number of people write vignettes in response to a common set of questions, their writing reveals dynamic practices because we can see the common elements that emerge across several stories as well as the complexities and specificity of each individual's story. In this book, therefore, we present teacher-leaders' vignettes to illustrate the nuances of how teachers learn to lead, and offer our own analysis of the themes about leadership learning that cut across these stories.

The Setting: National Writing Project

We chose to situate our project about teachers' leadership learning within the National Writing Project (NWP) because of its 35-year history of developing teachers as leaders (Gray, 2000; Lieberman & Wood, 2003; Stokes, 2005, 2010). The National Writing Project, founded by James Gray in 1974 with a single site and 29 participants including the director and codirectors, is a growing nationwide network of more than 200 local sites. It aims to improve the teaching of writing at all grade levels, kindergarten through college. Local Writing Project sites are housed on university campuses and codirected by university and K–12 faculty. Annually, across the nation, 3,000 teachers participate in leadership development opportunities through Summer Invitational Institutes and then serve nearly 100,000 educators by providing inservice professional development through their local Writing Project sites.

Writing Project sites follow a common model, adhering to a set of shared principles and practices for teachers' professional development and offering core programs that are common across the network. A set of basic principles serves as the foundation for the model:

- Writing can and should be taught, not just assigned, in every discipline and at every level of schooling.
- Teachers of writing must write.
- Effective professional development programs provide frequent opportunities for teachers to collectively and systematically examine research and practice.
- Teachers at every level—from kindergarten to college—are the agents of reform; universities and schools are ideal partners for investing together in that reform.
- Although there is no single right approach to teaching writing, some practices are better than others, and a research-informed community of practice is in the best position to design and develop a comprehensive writing program.

(McDonald, Buchanan, & Sterling, 2004)

For our study, one additional NWP principle is crucial: teachers who are well informed about pedagogy, content, and how students and teachers learn, and are effective in their classrooms are the best teachers of other teachers. Indeed, NWP is often referred to as the "teachers teaching teachers" model of professional development.

Through a set of core programs that reflect the Writing Project's mission and principles, known as the NWP model, sites support teachers in developing as leaders. Sites facilitate three major types of core programs. First, the intensive month-long *Invitational Institute* develops each site's cadre of teacher-consultants (i.e., those who have completed the institute). Sites seek out local teachers who demonstrate accomplished teaching, who are open to continued study, and who have potential as leaders. In the Invitational Institutes, Writing Project sites enact a set of social practices (Lieberman & Wood, 2003) that facilitate the development of a strong community and support teachers in seeing themselves as writers and leaders (Stokes, 2005, 2010; Whitney, 2008). Second, sites offer *Continuity* programs comprising a range of activities designed to support teacher-consultants in their ongoing development as classroom teachers and as professional development leaders following the Invitational Institute. Finally, *Inservice* programs, in the NWP lexicon, embrace a wide variety of programs that are designed and offered by the sites for teachers and schools in their service areas. All Inservice programs are led by the sites' teacher-consultants and provide leadership opportunities for these accomplished individuals. Collectively, these and other locally designed activities facilitate participating teachers' growth and development as leaders in the Writing Project as well as in their own schools and communities.

Learning from Teacher-Leaders:
Vignette Writing and Focus Group Interviews

We met with the 31 vignette writers for two writing retreats, each lasting 2½ days. (See the Appendix for a description of how we selected the vignette writers.) During the first retreat, we explained to the assembled teacher-leaders that we wanted them to write about their leadership by selecting a series of activities—less than a case, but more than one event—that "showed" rather than "told" how they were learning to lead. We asked the writers to develop their vignettes in response to a common prompt (see Figure 1). The retreat marked the beginning of a process of co-constructing the vignettes (Friedrich, Lieberman, & Hall, 2009). At this retreat, we worked with the teacher-leaders one-on-one and in writing response groups to choose one slice of their work, offering guidance about what topics seemed particularly well suited for this study.

In the 4 months between the retreats, each person created at least two drafts of his or her vignette and received written responses from one lead researcher.* In our responses, we asked them to elaborate what they did, to focus their stories, and to make explicit their leadership and the ways in which they learned to lead in the situation described.

---

*Ann Lieberman, Linda Friedrich, and Liza Percer served as the lead researchers during the vignette writing and interviewing phase of the project.

Figure 1. Vignette Prompt

We are doing a study of the leadership work of Writing Project teacher-consultants. We are looking at what teacher-consultants do, the content of their work, how teacher-consultants develop and get supported in their work with colleagues, their systems, and their students.

In no more than five pages, tell us about a concrete example of your work with colleagues, your school, your writing project site, your school district, or any other context that has occurred recently or in the past year. It may be a situation that includes a set of activities that took time to unfold.

Tell us a story of this situation, framing it by using the guidelines below.

Describe:

- What you were hoping would happen or be accomplished
- The context within which the work occurred
- What was involved
- The impact of the work
- Why you think it happened
- The role you played
- What feels most important about this work for you and why

At the second writing retreat, the teacher-leaders shared their works-in-progress with us and with their colleagues. Often, hearing others' stories and listening to the questions of their peers prompted them to add nuances to their stories and to clarify information about the context in which they worked. Following the second retreat, the writers received one final round of response and polished their vignettes. We further edited the vignettes included in our book. The vignette authors read, responded to, and approved our edits.

In addition to collecting vignettes, we invited the writers to participate in focus-group interviews near the end of the writing process. In groups of five or six, we asked the writers to 1. define what teacher leadership meant to them, 2. tell us whether they felt the term *leadership* applied to their work, and 3. reflect on whether writing their vignettes had shaped their views about leadership. What we learned helped us interpret the vignettes and illustrate these teacher-leaders' views on leadership throughout this book.

Our Analysis: Learning from the Vignettes

The full power of the vignettes becomes visible as we look across all 31 teacher-leaders' stories. To understand what the vignettes can tell us about how teachers learn to lead, we each read the vignettes several times, making notes about the ideas that emerged. We shared our ideas and agreed on a small number of themes, after which we reread all of the vignettes to identify those that provided the most insight into each theme. We then chose three or four vignettes to include in this book, based on how clearly each vignette illustrates the theme, whether the experiences described are broadly applicable within education, and the quality of the writing.

Once we identified our themes, we turned to the empirical and theoretical research literature. The literature prompted us to pose new questions about the vignettes, and we worked to draw connections between the literature and the writers' experiences and insights. After reading and synthesizing relevant literature, we once again read the vignettes related to the theme and generated findings related to each theme.

ORGANIZATION OF THE BOOK

We organized the book's chapters around four ideas central to teachers' leadership learning: identity, community, productive conflict, and practice. We open each chapter with a short summary of key research pieces, drawing on a broad range of theoretical and empirical literature. We then share three or four vignettes, relevant to the theme, in full to give readers a more complete picture of these vignette authors' leadership learning experiences. Each chapter concludes with our analysis of how the vignettes relate to the chapter's theme, citing examples from the full vignette collection. We draw examples from all the vignettes, including some not included in the book, in order to provide more nuance to our understanding of how teachers learn to lead. The Appendix includes a table that summarizes background information about the authors of the included vignettes to provide context for their stories.

Chapter 1, "Learning Leadership: Acquiring an Identity," draws on sociocultural theories of identity development to frame our analysis of how teachers develop identities as leaders over time and as they accept new roles. We consider how these teacher-leaders balance multiple identities and, as relevant, how the social identities of race and gender play into their leadership work. We include four vignettes in this chapter.

Chapter 2, "Learning to Build Collegiality and Community," provides a historical overview of empirical literature related to questions of collegiality, collaboration, and community in school-based settings—a central component of educational leaders' work. Here we analyze how participation in the Writing Project supported the teacher-leaders who participated in our project in learning how to create collaborative settings in which teachers and other professionals can learn from each other. We include three vignettes in this chapter.

Chapter 3, "Learning to Make Conflict Productive," draws on theories from the conflict resolution literature to examine the sources of conflicts, including power and social identity, and approaches to transforming conflict into productive learning opportunities. Resolving conflicts is a key leadership skill in education, so the chapter examines how selected literature in education and the vignettes address this issue. The chapter includes three vignettes.

Chapter 4, "Reflecting on New and Old Knowledge to Learn from Practice," summarizes key ideas from sociocultural theory about how people in a variety of fields learn from their day-to-day practice. It also examines how practitioner inquiry and research can facilitate educators' ongoing learning. We use these ideas to analyze how the vignette authors learn from their experiences as teachers and as leaders. The chapter includes four vignettes.

We conclude the book with a brief Epilogue. There we summarize how this work helps us reframe teacher leadership, examine how network participation contributes to leadership development, and discuss how academic research and teacher knowledge each contribute to a robust knowledge base for education.

Through our analysis and through the teacher-leaders' own stories, this book illustrates how teacher-leaders work day-to-day to improve teaching and student learning. The 14 vignettes included in this volume show the passionate commitment of these educators to students and to equity. We envision teacher-educators, professional developers, and teachers using our essays and the vignettes to prompt discussion about how to support teachers' development as leaders. In addition, we see the vignettes as starting points for discussing and writing about the dilemmas, challenges, and conflicts that educational leaders face. We have learned that asking teacher-leaders to write about their own work helps us all understand the complexities of teaching, learning, and leading.

Chapter 1

Learning Leadership: Acquiring an Identity

> [W]hen we first started this [vignette writing] process . . . I grappled with
> the word *leader*, because I didn't feel like I was a leader in my classroom
> in the traditional sense where I stood in front of the classroom and told
> [the students] what to do and they did it. We were all in it together. We
> were our own little community together, and I was the facilitator. (Re-
> tired teacher, June 2006)

Today roles for teacher-leaders, as well as openings for formal leadership
positions, are rapidly expanding. Fresh thinking about "distributed leadership" (Spillane, 2006; Spillane & Diamond, 2007), newly defined roles
for principals and teachers (Sergiovanni, 2004), and calls for nurturing
and developing teacher-leaders (Lieberman & Miller, 2004) open up possibilities for constructing these leadership positions in different ways. Many
teachers, however, continue to be reluctant to claim the title and identity
of leader.

Teachers' reluctance stems in part from persistent, widely held ideas
that define leadership as working hierarchically, having all the answers, and
holding power over others. Such approaches, which are reinforced by the
bureaucratic norms of schools and districts, clash with the collaborative approaches typically taken by teacher-leaders (Little, 1995; Smylie & Denny,
1990). Teachers hesitate to call themselves leaders because the egalitarian
culture of schools treats all teachers as being the same and school administrators as having more authority (Lortie, 1975). In other words, although
teachers may view each other differently based on their years of experience, teachers are teachers; they are not administrators. Teachers fear being
perceived as bragging when they share information about their practice.
And teachers who decide to step into formal leadership positions, such as
assistant principal or district administrator, risk rejection, isolation, and resistance from their former peers. So how and why do some teachers come
not only to accept the responsibility of leadership, but also to claim this
identity? And why does this matter?

In this chapter we draw on sociocultural theories of identity development
to help us understand how the teacher-leaders whom we studied came to
see and present themselves as leaders despite education's cultural norms. The

theoretical literature, developed outside education and referenced in the next section of this chapter, investigates the ways in which identities develop and shift over time and the role that well-established cultural and organizational expectations play in shaping individuals' identities and actions. Virtually all of the vignettes address issues related to developing a leadership identity. Following the summary of relevant literature, we share four vignettes that illustrate this theme. We conclude the chapter with our analysis of how teachers form, claim, and reconcile their identities as leaders, drawing examples from the four vignettes we have included as well as from others.

SOCIOCULTURAL THEORIES OF IDENTITY

Sociologists, anthropologists, and psychologists all study how people form identities—in occupational roles, as members of cultural and social groups, as participants in organizations or informal social groups. Over the past 3 decades, sociologists and anthropologists have increasingly drawn on sociocultural theories of learning (e.g., Vygotsky, 1978) to explain how people come to see themselves and each other, and how these identities shape their actions. These theorists suggest that individuals develop their identities through day-to-day interactions, *and* that widely held societal and cultural definitions shape how we see ourselves and our place in the world. They explain why developing a particular identity matters:

> [I]dentifying oneself as an agent in the system—an actor in the world as defined by the game—is a necessary precursor to mastering the system beyond a certain level. One has to develop a concept of oneself in the activity and want either to realize that self or to avoid it. (Holland, Lachiotte Jr., Skinner, & Cain, 1998, pp. 119–120)

In other words, how individuals see themselves shapes their ability to participate in social activities including work, relationships, and religious and community commitments. At the same time, individuals choose and shape the activities they pursue.

To understand this idea in relation to education, consider a teacher who has recently stepped into an administrative position. In the words of one researcher, "Perhaps the most difficult challenge that the beginning school administrator faces . . . is the need to develop a professional identity—'an image of self' as a proactive leader who can make a difference (Ronkowski & Iannaccone, 1989)" (Normore, 2004, p. 112). This statement illustrates how seeing oneself differently—in this case as a proactive leader—shapes the individual's ability to serve effectively.

We primarily draw ideas about identity development relevant to teacher leadership from two sources. The first is Wenger's (1998) *Communities of Practice: Learning, Meaning, and Identity*. Wenger builds his theory of identity formation on a case study of an insurance claims processing unit. He articulates how individuals develop their identities as members of communities of practice, defined as spaces where people collectively create the practices they use every day and interpret what happens around them. Identities develop through daily interactions with other members of the community as well as with those outside of it. They also get shaped by the larger social landscape and artifacts of practice (e.g., policies). However, this is not a one-way process; individuals also shape the meanings and activities of their local community of practice.

Our second set of ideas about identity is presented in Holland, Lacchiote, Jr., Skinner, and Cain's (1998) *Identity and Agency in Cultural Worlds*. Their theory of identity formation seeks to integrate theories arguing that culture dictates identity and action with social constructivist theories that suggest identity is improvised through ongoing interactions. They conclude that individuals' identities and sense of ability to act do not come from within but are shaped by their use of and response to cultural norms and givens. Seeking to understand "identities in practice" (p. 271), the authors argue that identity, expertise, and the worlds in which these phenomena exist codevelop over time.

Our analysis of the four vignettes in this chapter, which follows the vignettes, shows how social identity theories can inform our understanding of how leadership identity develops for teachers. Three key ideas taken from these theories guided our analysis:

1. Identity is not fixed, but is constantly being negotiated. Individuals hold multiple, sometimes competing, ideas or conceptions of the self, which arise in part because of their participation in many social circles over time. While we don't believe that individuals must form a single, unitary identity, we do recognize that individuals expend energy "reconciling" their multiple conceptions of self (Wenger, 1998).
2. Identity is inherently social; it involves both how we see ourselves and how others perceive us. Identity develops through socialization processes and ongoing daily interactions. Although identity is negotiable, it is also informed and constrained by preexisting cultural expectations, occupational role definitions, historical forces, and an individual's position vis-à-vis enduring social categories of race, gender, and social class (for further discussion of these ideas see, for example, Galindo, Aragon, & Underhill, 1996; Gutierrez & Rogoff, 2003; Holvino, 2001).

3. While our conceptions of self are informed and constrained by larger social forces, there can still be room for change in what Holland and her colleagues (1998) refer to as "the space of authoring" (p. 169). There, individuals make sense of and respond to these larger social forces. In addition, changes both in individual identity and in larger social patterns are made possible through "making worlds" (p. 272).

FORGING LEADERSHIP IDENTITIES: TEACHER-LEADERS' VOICES

For teachers, claiming an identity as a leader matters because it opens up possibilities for contributing not only to their own students but also to other educators. In this section we present four vignettes (each preceded by brief contextual information) that highlight different dimensions of how teachers develop and claim their identities as leaders.

Austen Reilley, *a middle school English language arts teacher, developed her identity as a teacher and a leader while working to create single-gender spaces for writing in her rural school. She showed how her identity changed over time as she encountered both positive and negative experiences. Although she spent her first 2 years in an urban charter school, Reilley's identity as a teacher and a leader began to grow when she moved to her present school, located in a small university town surrounded by rural areas in another state. Her school serves 600 students, 70% of whom receive free or reduced-price lunch and 98% of whom are Caucasian.*

RIPPLE-EFFECTIVE LEADERSHIP: TRANSFORMING PASSION INTO PLANS

Austen Reilley

My first 2 years as a teacher nearly killed my desire to teach. I was a brand new college graduate in a brand new K–12 public charter school that was trying to do very progressive and ambitious things for a community with a 90% dropout rate before the 12th grade. But there were very few structures in place to support the daily operations, and there was very little teaching going on. It was disillusionment boot camp. My family and friends could only watch me fold in on myself.

With each passing year, the experience of my first 2 years has become more valuable as a defining moment in my development as a teacher. I believe if I had not gotten away from that first chaotic environment by moving to a new school, I would not have been a teacher for even one more semester.

Connecting to something greater than ourselves, whether philosophical or spiritual, is crucial as educators, as is positive reinforcement when we do things right. But external support is not always offered or available. So, to what do we cling to keep the fire going?

For me, what keeps me coming back every day and every August is simple. I love to write. I crave the deep sense of satisfaction and calm it gives me. It is more than my content area; it is my passion. I rediscovered this passion in my first 2 years of teaching. During those years, I attended classes at a private organization in Cincinnati, Ohio, called Women Writing for (a) Change (WWf(a)C). I was in a Saturday morning class with women of varying ages and experiences whose only commonality was an interest in writing. We shared, voluntarily, what we wrote each class meeting. It was in these moments, hearing my voice speak my words to a room full of people, that I gained confidence as a writer and as a teacher. It was life changing.

As a writer, learner, and teacher, I need to think out loud, hear other peoples' thought processes, share what I know, write, and don't understand, in order to be successful. As a teacher, I am isolated from adult conversation for 90% of my day. My kids are all I've got. So I have gone about the business of trying to take this knowledge of "what lies within" myself and apply it to my teaching, so my students can have the same chance at a meaningful community of writers. In terms of leadership style, I guess this would be the distributive property school of thought: What works for me as a writer will more than likely work for my student writers.

When I started teaching seventh grade language arts in my current rural Kentucky school, I saw girls whose potential was buried, even to themselves, underneath insecurity, social priorities, body image issues—you name it. Middle school students deal daily with a host of issues that I would not wish on my worst adult enemy. In my classes, very few would share their writing or respond openly to others' writing. They were missing out. In my heart of hearts, I believed that, if the girls were by themselves, things would be different. I decided to try my own version of WWf(a)C, to give them a taste of what I loved so much. My principal was very supportive of the idea, and I got to work.

I made up fliers for the club, and recruited girls from my classes to spread the word to girls from other classes and grade levels. Out of sheer laziness I did not name the club, but this proved serendipitous later on. Sixth, seventh, and eighth graders applied, and everyone got in because the only criteria were gender and an interest in writing of any kind at any level. At our first meeting, I welcomed the girls. I told them why I wanted to try this club, and all about my experience at WWf(a)C. They looked at me like I was a crazy hippie (an easy leap since they knew I had grown up in California), and then we wrote. My first prompt suggestion was to list anything and everything about ourselves that was unique—good, bad, or neutral. I have since realized that middle school girls, like me, love to list things, name things, and be known.

Following the WWf(a)C model, we had time at the end of the session to go around the circle, and each girl shared if she wanted to. Not everyone shared, but most did. We learned everything, from grooming habits to the kinds of boys they liked. "This is turning out to be a good thing," I thought. It got better. They decided they needed to name the club, and that we should have a contest to pick the best name. The name that won unanimously also came with a slogan for possible t-shirts: "The Winged Writers: Pick up a pen and fly. . . ."

Success for these girls did not come in the form of quantitative data. However, those whom I saw during the school day did participate noticeably more in my classes, which could only help their learning. They expressed their personal gains as the freedom to be themselves, to write, to get to know girls they normally wouldn't, and to try new things. Some of them expressed these gains in writing, which they read at our first public read-around for their families and friends at the folk art museum in our town, and which, incidentally, made me cry in front of all those people. I think they took this as a great personal victory, and so did I.

Every Thursday afternoon for the past 4 years, Winged Writers has recharged my teaching battery. Being there reminds me that, though many of my students still don't like to write, some of them love it. It also crystallizes for me that my classes should follow the same model as closely as possible to create the same kind of community if I want my students to enjoy writing, write more, write better, give and receive better feedback, and grow as individuals.

My experiences with WWf(a)C and Winged Writers have made me a great believer in single-gender grouping as a valuable tool in the teaching of writing. After my first year with the Winged Writers, I started doing more research. I found a wealth of educational journal articles and news items featuring schools that had tried gender-specific classes, describing their results, including things like fewer discipline issues, better test scores, and higher morale. At our next yearly school-run test data analysis meeting, we discussed one of our most glaring achievement gaps: gender. Our girls are outperforming our boys at a significant rate—especially in writing.

I have to admit that, as a woman, a petty part of me loved to read these data; but the socially responsible teacher in me inferred that our boys obviously needed something different. I am clearly not the first one to realize this. I printed out some choice articles and passed them on to my principal and guidance counselors. My principal decided she would present some of this information to the site-based decision-making council and our district school board, both of whom approved her proposal for a pilot study of gender-specific language arts classes at the seventh-grade level. I was to teach an all-boys' class, and a colleague of mine would teach an all-girls' class. We would look at the data, and see what we thought. To my pleasant surprise, my boys' class was by far my favorite group on my schedule that year. This is not to say they were not challenging, but that I enjoy a challenge.

A classroom full of 12-year-old boys is the mother of invention. And not just mine, but theirs. From them, I learned the value of physical activity paired with learning, friendly competition, performance, explicit modeling of writing and conferring practices, and constant feedback. They forced me out of my shell on a daily basis, and my teaching will never be the same, luckily for me. The only "distinguished" scores among my students on the seventh-grade writing portfolio (part of Kentucky's state assessment of school progress) that year were earned by boys in that class, and there were very few "novice" scores from that group. Overall, the boys in that group outperformed boys in my mixed classes in terms of participation, portfolio scores, and (more important) general willingness to write. Our pilot study led to each teacher in our building having at least one single-gender class period in her schedule, and the seventh-grade language arts teachers having mostly single-gender classes, with the exception of a collaboration class with a special education teacher that, due to scheduling complexities, needed to be mixed gender.

I am not a person who has always known she wanted to be a teacher. In fact, in my 6th year of teaching, I'm still not positive I can see myself doing it until retirement age. The longer teachers stay in teaching, the more stories we have of individual kids who make it worthwhile, and lessons we know we have nailed, at least once. I have started to be able to imagine myself taking on more of a leadership role in my profession. I have heard people speak of following one's bliss in one's work, which I think, for me, is the intellectual exercise of figuring out what works for my students and for me. With the receptive response to new ideas I get from my school principal, the encouragement from my Writing Project director, and the community I feel immediately with other teacher-consultants I meet through the National Writing Project, I can value my own voice and what it has to say. That is what I will hang onto while I carry on with the grand experiment of being and becoming the teacher I am supposed to be.

Linda Tatman, *the assistant director of a graduate program for teachers, illustrated how she maintained her identity as a teacher as she transitioned from teaching high school to teaching teachers, thus reconciling multiple identities. In addition, she explored how she created a leadership role that emphasized collaboration rather than hierarchical relationships and showed how individuals may be able to change expectations for established roles. Tatman's program, which is housed in the university's English department and run by her local Writing Project site, engages teachers in taking online courses and conducting action research.*

FROM TEACHING TEENS TO TEACHING TEACHERS: FINDING A NEW VOICE

Linda Tatman

> The powerful play goes on and you can contribute a verse.
> —Walt Whitman (1900/2006)

Anticipation and anxiety—this ambivalence haunted me during the weeks after accepting the invitation to join the Ohio Writing Project team as an assistant director, managing our K–12 Master of Arts in Teaching (MAT) program and serving as its action research advisor for the high school candidates. Anticipation, because my previous affiliations with the Writing Project had always been positive. Anxiety, because I was nudging myself out of my comfort zone of working with students to working with teachers. My high school students and I had created a community of readers and writers—they felt safe taking risks. They made their needs and goals known through their writing and our classroom discussions. I was comfortable engaging them in reflective practice through questioning and modeling what I wanted them to learn.

But in my new leadership role, how was I going to parlay all of this into a situation with classroom teachers who, aside from interviews during the MAT process and an occasional classroom visit, would spend the preponderance of their time with me via the Internet? How could I possibly create and foster a community when we weren't together one-on-one daily? And another challenge—with so many of these teachers being younger, would my storehouse of teaching strategies appear as revolutionary as they had to me after my initial Ohio Writing Project workshops? Would I have anything new to offer? Finally, would I be able to approach these teachers in the same way I did my students? I used inquiry to guide my sophomores and seniors, urging them to find answers for themselves—answers that worked for them. I encouraged them to think critically and to engage in reflection. Could I do the same with these teachers?

Once I was settled into my position the following September, interviews with prospective MAT candidates ensued. I found these meetings to be a good venue for getting to know these K–12 teachers and learning what they needed for themselves and for their students. And were those interviews fruitful! Of course, I wanted to know everything—how they like teaching, what texts they use in their classes, how their students feel about reading and writing, what concerns, needs, and goals they have—the final questions always serving as a segue for the opening of the proverbial flood gates with ones of their own. Each teacher left the interviews with hope and excitement, and I left feeling as if we had begun to create our community.

I also left with their stories and questions to share with my fellow action research advisors as we collaboratively designed our online classes. We talked about how to engage in online exchanges to make them more personal so we could foster community, so we could build a trusting relationship. We generated questions for our assignments that would invite our teachers to think about what they are doing in their classrooms and why. Finally, we talked about how we could offer ideas based on our own teaching experiences so that they could revisit them with their own students.

The responses from my high school teachers' assignments during our online chats revealed as much about their struggles as they did about their successes:

> "I'm still grappling with using essential questions to frame a unit of study!"
> "I need some ideas to help my freshmen with their independent reading!"
> "My students just aren't getting the idea of revision . . . what should I do?"
> "Help! I'm having a hard time finding a new way to teach the research paper!"
> "I need more ideas to get my boys started with their writing!"

On the positive side, they were finding that using rubrics for assessing assignments was working well, and so was modeling writing-craft lessons, writing along with their students, and creating a community of writers in their own classrooms. I found myself reading and rereading each of their e-mail correspondences, making notes in the margins about what they were asking, what they needed and wanted, and what I had in my boxes of teaching materials from my own experiences to share with them. And of course I contemplated how to show my ideas without coming right out and telling them that this is what I did that worked, so it should work for them.

I pulled together lessons and resources on essential questions that I had used with my *Romeo and Juliet* unit and suggested that one teacher frame her own with questions about family responsibility, love at first sight, and the element of fate. For the teacher who had questions regarding independent reading, I mentioned Harvey Daniels and his texts about literature circles, and we began discussing how this teaching method might offer her the accountability she was seeking. I even sent one of my assignments to review and remodel. And, for the teacher whose boys seemed constantly reluctant to put pen to paper, we explored many ways to get them started, including the suggestion of using writing marathons to generate ideas for their writing journals.

Through this process, I began to realize that the classroom practices and sources I had used weren't that familiar after all. I did have new and useful ideas to contribute. Because I was really listening, responding to what each needed, and showing them that we were "in this together," they felt comfortable and were ready to step out and try new things with their students. Finally, because I asked questions about incorporating new strategies and texts rather than merely telling them what to do, they were better able to think, evaluate, and reflect. They felt that I had given them permission to take what I had to offer and rework it to meet their needs.

During one monthly class led by our Ohio Writing Project director, Dr. Mary Fuller, our teachers shared topics and pieces of their research. And just when we thought this class session was about to come to a close, something unexpected occurred. These teachers began expressing how our Ohio Writing Project workshops and MAT program had given them the confidence and knowledge to become better writers and teachers.

This new leadership role as assistant director has taught me that I can make a difference with these classroom teachers. We *can* have that community like the ones we create with our students, even if it isn't always face-to-face. We *can* and *need* to offer each other support because teachers so often work in isolation behind the closed doors of our classrooms. We *need* a network of ideas and resources, and we need a confirmation that we're doing what's best for our students beyond their test scores. And we can have it—it's right here at the Ohio Writing Project.

Teaching, as well as life, is a powerful play; and in a very real way, so is the MAT program at the Ohio Writing Project. And we all have verses to contribute. I had them for my students about good writing; I now have them for my MAT teachers about good teaching. In my present journey with the Ohio Writing Project, I have found my voice with helping other teachers. I am working with a new MAT class, and there will be another and another as the years pass. And I know each group will come with a new set of struggles. My confidence to face these, however, has grown. I now say, "Bring them on"—because new struggles will lead to new verses. And the powerful play will go on.

Yarda Leflet, *a high school assistant principal, learned to stay true to her principles and negotiated teachers' changing expectations of her as she transitioned from serving as an English teacher to becoming an administrator. In her vignette, which is written in the form of a journal, she illustrated the social nature of identity development by describing teachers' reactions and her responses. At the time she became an assistant principal, Leflet's suburban high school served 1,800 students, of whom 51% were Caucasian, 45% Hispanic, and 3% African American. Of the students, 27% were categorized as economically disadvantaged and 3% as Limited English Proficient.*

KICKED OUT OF THE CLUB:
LEARNING FROM MAKING THE TRANSITION FROM TEACHER TO PRINCIPAL

Yarda Leflet

MARCH 2005: THE INVITATION

My principal informs me that one of the assistant principals is leaving, and he thinks I should consider applying for the position. He thinks I would do a great job. I am in shock, honored, and speechless. He shows me the job description and asks me to submit my résumé. I notice the list of duties on the job description is extensive. The position is for an instructional assistant principal. I tell him I will talk it over with my husband and let him know tomorrow.

Me, an administrator? Sure, I have talked about how I wanted to become an administrator someday, but I didn't think the opportunity would come this soon. In 2002 I went through the district's Leadership Institute, founded to help the district build leadership capacity as it confronted rapid growth and a shortage of strong principal applicants, thinking someday in the future I would want to be an administrator. At the institute I learned about leadership styles, team building, monitoring the curriculum, effective decision-making models, and schoolwide change.

What about my current job? I love being English department chair. And I love working half time with central office on English language arts curriculum. I love trying to empower teachers by allowing them opportunities to learn, grow, and develop innovative and creative techniques to improve student learning. My department shares ideas, is interested in staff development, and is truly working to improve student achievement. I love my work with the Central Texas Writing Project. Can I even continue to work with the Central Texas Writing Project as an AP? I don't know anyone with CTWP who is an administrator. Most of all, I love my students. I will miss them terribly if I leave the classroom. So, why make the change?

APRIL 2005: "YOU ARE NOT A TEACHER"

Here I sit as the English department chair with the special education department chair, the other three core department chairs, one AP, and the academic dean. We are writing our campus improvement plan for 2005–2006. We are called the "magnificent seven." For the most part I just listen. We start to make a list of suggestions. I make one suggestion and am told, "Yarda, that is fine for you to suggest, but you are not a teacher. You are one of them. As a teacher I don't think this is something we can do." I am stunned. I am teaching classes just like every other teacher on this campus. I do my grades, call parents, and plan with other teachers in my department. I want to shout,

"I am a teacher on this campus. I have been for 7 years." But I don't. I just sit quietly through the rest of the meeting and keep my thoughts to myself. I was put in my place. People have been isolating me lately. I'm not invited to go eat; I am not a part of the daily conversations. Everyone is silent when I walk in a room. I know they were talking before I walked in. Tell me, why did I choose to become an administrator? My husband and I were joking about it last night. He told me I have been kicked out of the club. It makes me sad; my feelngs are hurt. I will definitely need to grow tougher skin to do this job.

AUGUST 2005: MY FIRST MONTH AS ASSISTANT PRINCIPAL

I keep telling myself I am the same person I have always been. However, it seems the world around me has changed its expectations. Before this year I was in the background—I facilitated, collaborated, provided teachers in my department things they needed, worked with curriculum, scheduled professional development, and helped empower teachers. I feel I still do all of these things, but it seems much different.

Professional development now is with the entire faculty in stadium-style seating—by PowerPoint. I talk, they listen—this is not what I have always done. Teachers wait for me to give them direction, or give the answers they think I want to hear. I used to be seen as an expert in curriculum, but now I am portrayed as someone who just doesn't understand what it is like to teach. I want to open doors to teachers to help them. How do I do this now? I am truly not part of the teacher club anymore. However, I am not yet part of the administrator club either.

OCTOBER 2005: COLLABORATING WITH TEACHERS, AGAIN

I conducted a half-day training on sheltered instruction today. I was able to do the training by department, not in stadium seats. At the end, I had everyone sit in a circle and brainstorm about how they thought we could better meet the needs of these students. At first each group was reluctant. Then they just started to pour out ideas—great ideas. About 15 minutes into one discussion our academic dean walked in. Silence. She left. They all looked at me and started to talk again. I was part of their learning community. We were there to try to improve our school together. And I admit, I loved it.

NOVEMBER 2005: STAYING CONNECTED WITH THE WRITING PROJECT

I want to go to the National Writing Project Annual Meeting. My principal tells me, "Yarda, this is the last time you need to go to a conference for ELA stuff." He has always been supportive of my involvement with the National Writing Project. Now as an AP, even an instructional AP, it just isn't as acceptable for me to be involved. I explained what our partnership with the local NWP site had done for our school. Our scores on the state assessment went up significantly. Our teachers now feel more confident teaching writing, and they are using best practices. And now, our grants are done. We have no money for substitutes for planning, for teachers to attend conferences, for books to conduct book studies. Our scores have not increased significantly since the grant ran out. When I left his office, I think he understood.

FEBRUARY 2006: WRITING AND REFLECTING

In order to define the line between teacher-leader and principal I have minimal interaction with the English department I had been a part of for 8 years. "You need to think like a principal, not an English teacher," I am told. Although I work a little bit with all departments, I am *not* the supervisor for the English depart- ment but instead for the math department—a department that thinks I am going to "infect" them with writing. Maybe I will. I need to write again even though this is not something that is seen as important in my current job. I still keep wondering though, "How do administrators reflect on their practice without writing?" Maybe it is up to me to show the value of reflection and writing in ad- ministration. I just need to stay true to myself and the National Writing Project and continue to learn and teach teachers the way I know to be the best. After all, if I continue to write, maybe students, teachers, and principals will follow.

JUNE 2006: FACILITATING COLLABORATIVELY

The principal, every department chair, all assistant principals, and I are working on the 2006–2007 campus improvement plan. How are we going to increase the level of rigor, relevance, relationships, and responsibility on our campus? The principal leads us into a brainstorming session of the R words that our cam- pus should concentrate on. It turns out to be quite comical and sets a positive mood for the day. What is needed on our campus? I want to hear from each committee member—what do they really think? We work on focusing our vision for next year. The first 2 hours are filled with laughter, silence, and frustration as we have real conversations about the state of our school. Instead of making a suggestion right away, I sit and listen—making notes about what teachers are saying. I ask questions, restate what they say, and help the principal facilitate the discussion. I am pushing them to be better. One department chair asks me what I think. I am filled with excitement and explain my thoughts on the topic. They ask me questions, restate what I have said, and push me back—force me to take it to the next level. We all expect a lot from each other and from our campus next year. We don't leave for lunch—we all eat together, everyone smil- ing the entire time. We talk about how to build learning communities for our teachers, how to have more effective teams on campus and programs to start to offer students help. We talk a lot about the students—student achievement, instructional strategies for meeting the needs of all students, what students really need, and our school culture.

As I leave the meeting at the end of the day, I think how fortunate I am to work with such wonderful people each and every day. They value my opinion and I value theirs, and we can have real conversations about our school without anyone becoming judgmental. We have a principal who truly believes it takes each and every one of us to make our campus great—and she articulates it on a daily basis. My campus is my family—students to principals, custodians to teachers, each and every person on my campus—and I love it.

NOVEMBER 2009: LOOKING BACK AT MY CHANGED ROLE

As I look back on becoming an assistant principal, I can now see why my relationship with members of the school's leadership changed. When I first accepted my new appointment in the spring of 2005, I didn't know how to approach the meeting as a new administrator. I approached it as a teacher and wanted to participate just as I had always done.

Over my first year as an administrator, I earned the respect of the faculty and staff, thus creating a more positive environment. I realized as a leader I needed to first really listen to my staff and not interject my own opinions first. By really listening, I was able to eliminate some of the teacher/administrator barriers, build time for reflection, and show that I am committed to students, to student learning, and to them as professionals. As soon as I had demonstrated this, we were able to truly collaborate to make the school better.

Elizabeth A. Davis, *a technology teacher in an urban middle school, engaged her students in social action projects and in that process developed her own capacities as a teacher-leader. She illustrated how she and her students developed a sense of agency despite social constraints and expectations. Of the students served by Davis's former middle school, 77% are eligible for free and reduced-price lunch and 99% are African American.*

TEACHER LEADERSHIP THROUGH WRITING AND BUILDING ALLIANCES

Elizabeth A. Davis

Like Brazilian educator Paulo Freire (Freire & Macedo, 1987), I believe that teachers should "live part of their dreams within their educational space"

(p. 127). Therefore I create a laboratory for initiating social action and social justice thinking in my classroom. I don't believe that teachers are neutral. I share, but don't impose, my beliefs to help students raise critical questions and find their own solutions to problems. Teachers do not have to acquiesce to the notion that lessons connected to students' lives and lived experiences compromise content rigor or high expectations for academic achievement. Instead, students' lives are a valuable part of the text.

I began my lifelong career as a civil rights activist during my 3 years as a student at Eastern Senior High School when I joined the Modern Strivers, the school district's first Black student union. I continue my activism as a teacher by modeling the power of writing and building alliances, as well as by opening up opportunities for students to advocate for themselves. Part of my dream as an educator is to make my classroom a laboratory for equity and social justice.

CONNECTING IDENTITY, COMMUNITY, AND LEARNING

I have learned from my students that achieving a sense of self-identity is a principal focal point of middle school and that what I teach in my classroom is not the only factor contributing to its development. They have also taught me about the other three "R's" of schooling—resistance, revolution, and rising up. These generally occurred in my classroom when the lessons were disconnected from students' lives and community. This is why I eventually invited my students to bring their lives, along with the other required tools and materials, into my classroom.

The 50th anniversary of *Brown v. Board of Education* provided an unexpected opportunity to connect my students' lives with local and national history and social action. I had been teaching at Sousa Middle School for 6 years when I learned about its rich history from a brief article appearing in the Metro section of the *Washington Post*. I shared the article with students and staff, who knew only that our school was named after a bandleader. The *Bolling v. Sharpe* case introduced Sousa's students to Linda Brown, Homer Plessy, Thurgood Marshall, and Spottswood Thomas Bolling, a 12-year-old Black boy, later discovered to have also been a "block boy," who rose up, resisted injustice, and started a revolution against racial segregation in the public schools of the District of Columbia. But more importantly, when Sousa's students began reading, writing, and critically thinking about these cases, they discovered that the avenues Spottswood Bolling used over 50 years ago to resolve his school problem required the same resources needed to address their current issues—parent, student, and community power.

Ensuring that my students knew the history and significance of these cases was only the tip of the iceberg. My most important objective for taking them into this piece of civil rights history was to find solutions to the current problems they were facing at Sousa and in their community. My students and I received multiple requests to speak about conditions at Sousa because of the school's connection to the *Brown v. Board* case. The requests came from members of the Congressional Black Caucus and the United States Senate, Court TV and C-Span, as well as community organizations.

I worked with my students to write and revise their testimonies for these audiences. Kendra (a pseudonym) developed her testimony during my students' investigation into *Bolling v. Sharpe*. She highlighted the fact that 50 years after Brown, Sousa was still racially segregated and still not equal to public schools in northwestern DC. She addressed the dual school system that still exists due to resegregation and gentrification. I had not prepared a written statement but was unexpectedly asked to speak. I recall pointing out my caution, while teaching about *Brown*, not to send the message that my students could only learn in schools with White children or teachers, even though money and resources seemed to follow White children. I strongly suspected that my students' televised testimony prompted the donation of $5,000 and books for classroom libraries at Sousa. These acts were testaments to me and my students that at least some of the power to change circumstances in our lives was vested in us.

Our *Bolling v. Sharpe* investigation not only garnered donations of library books, it saved Sousa from the wrecking ball. My students petitioned their classmates, teachers, parents, community members, and school board to halt the demolition and preserve the school's status as a historical landmark.

The school is now undergoing a 2-year modernization process. During the first year of the renovations, however, the district housed students and staff in a barely habitable wing of the school, unused for 15 years. In 2005–2006, our tasks included advocacy for moving to a safe temporary space.

BUILDING COMMUNITY ALLIANCES

In the process of helping my students develop their democratic capacities to enact change, I have developed my own as a teacher-leader. The more passionate I became about these issues, the more supports I needed. The list of supports expanded beyond the boundaries of my classroom, the school, and the school system. In many cases, the leadership roles that emerged for me required greater and riskier responsibilities and a broader vision of the supports needed to change unsatisfactory conditions. Our work at Sousa opened doors for forging new alliances.

In the last week of school during *Brown's* 50th anniversary year, my students shared Sousa's story and their social action project with over 50 high school students from DC and the surrounding jurisdictions. The leading candidate for the neighborhood's city council seat attended the session. His passion for public education and his comments to the students made such an impression on me that I later organized a dinner meeting between him and the 457 DC Public Schools (DCPS) teachers living in his district.

The alliances that I forged with this city council member have been help-ful in my students' and my efforts to move the school to a clean, safe space during the remainder of the renovation process. I called on him to visit the school after the process had begun. He came with the city council chairper-son to do a walk-through. When they visited my classroom, I asked for their assessment and both agreed that it was not an environment conducive to learning. After 1 school year, the board of education finally agreed to move the students and staff into a temporary space outside the building for the remainder of the modernization process.

EXPANDING BEYOND SOUSA

When the School Modernization Bill was introduced to the city council, Sousa was already on the list of schools to be modernized. But the bill was a golden opportunity to engage Sousa's students in a social action process beyond their own school and community. Like Sousa Middle School, over 100 DC public schools were more than a half-century-old, with crumbling in-frastructures that could not support the newest technologies needed to meet the district's standards of learning. Hundreds of students had been forced to leave their communities in search of schools in other neighborhoods. When students began to understand that the bill would address all of the district's crumbling schools, they also realized that they could attend a modernized, well-resourced high school in their own community. Reading, writing, and thinking about the bill helped them to connect the dots in their learning about their social and fiscal responsibility in solving problems and enacting change in their lives.

At the time, the mayor and city council had already agreed to build a $600 million baseball stadium in the shadow of my crumbling alma mater. During this time, I had affiliated with three public school support groups. Each planned its own strategies and activities to get the bill passed. I planned ways to engage my students in all of them. When one group staged a demonstra-tion at the baseball stadium, my students and their parents were there with speeches and placards.

I required my students to write letters to their parents about the bill and the activities planned in support of getting it passed. The students drafted a petition letter to the members on the City Council Education Committee and collected over 400 petition letters from parents. They delivered these during the public hearing for the School Modernization Bill.

The campaign began to attract hundreds of supporters, including pro-fessional organizers and campaign strategists. Our campaign chairman, who initiated strategic campaigns for the Teamsters Union, thought it would be beneficial for DCPS award-winning teachers to stage a press conference out-side one of the oldest schools in the city to show the support of DC public school teachers for the bill. The press conference was a huge success. Three major news networks showed up to cover the story. The bill was voted out of the council's education committee and passed by the full council.

The petition letter-writing campaign and supporting actions not only had a direct impact on school modernization, but also resulted in the building of powerful alliances with parents, community members, and organizations. The students' activities inspired other teachers and students to carry out similar projects. This work builds on my 32-year history as an educator and public education advocate who aspires to make my classroom a laboratory for social justice. It has become the fuel for my energy to teach.

After the press conference and my appearance as a speaker at various council, board, and community meetings, my image as a teacher concerned about the conditions needed to support quality teaching and learning began to develop into that of a community organizer and political activist. While this may have served the groups with which I was affiliated, it did not serve me well as a public school teacher. Local school leaders were leery of teachers who spoke up or spoke out about unjust conditions in "their" schools. My reputation as a social justice teacher was magically transformed into that of an agitator. While such teachers may be hailed by parents and teachers as heroes or heroines, they are personae non gratae to local school leaders in schools that facilitate maintaining the status quo.

WHAT IS TEACHER LEADERSHIP?

Although many of my colleagues perceive me as a teacher-leader, I have avoided wearing the label because of my own perceptions of teacher-leaders who had been ordained as leaders by local school administrators who wanted "servant" leaders who would become extensions of themselves. Over the years, I have learned that teacher-leaders are both self- and other-appointed. Some teachers are leaders in their local schools, while others are perceived as leaders outside of their local schools and school districts. Over the years, I have worked hard to become both.

HOW TEACHERS DEVELOP LEADERSHIP IDENTITIES: OUR ANALYSIS

Almost all the vignette writers described themselves as both teachers and leaders. This pattern held true no matter whether the writer had continued to serve as a classroom teacher or taken a position as an administrator. While

this pattern resonates with a common refrain that we hear from educators—
"I'm just a teacher"—it contrasts with some literature that suggests that
administrators need to leave their teacher identities behind and adopt new
singular identities as principals or district personnel (c.f., Browne-Ferringo,
2003; Crow & Glascock, 1995). Hence we now use examples from the four
vignettes presented in the preceding section, as well as other vignettes not
presented in this book, to illustrate how the writers developed both their
formal and informal identities as leaders. In particular, we explore how the
writers reconcile their identities as teachers and as leaders and in the process
develop a new vision for leadership.

Creating and Reconciling Multiple Identities Across Time

Identities constantly change, sometimes subtly and sometimes dramatically.
Identity is not developed early on and then simply maintained (Wenger,
1998). The vignette writers show us how their identities as educators and as
leaders gradually unfold and develop nuances over time. They also emphasize the multidimensional nature of identity.

Codeveloping Expertise and Identity. Individual expertise and identification with a particular practice or role develop together. Lave and Wenger
(1991) refer to this process of becoming a member of a particular community of practice as "legitimate peripheral participation," while Holland
and her colleagues (1998) describe it as "codevelopment." To illustrate how
teachers codevelop their leadership practices and identities, we analyze vignettes from two classroom teachers—one early in her career, one a veteran.

Austen Reilley, a middle school teacher, showed how her professional
identity continued to develop during her first 6 years in teaching. Her
vignette illustrates how seeing oneself as an agent supports an individual
in developing expertise and simultaneously shows how experience can
lead individuals both to question and to embrace their identities. Her first
2 years of teaching in a chaotic environment, where she received limited
support "nearly killed [her] desire to teach" and prompted her to question
her identity as a teacher. However, writing sustained her and she drew
upon her passion for writing to help her become a better teacher in her
next school. By engaging her students in the kinds of writing activities that
had worked for her, she started experiencing success as a teacher. Reilley's
positive outcomes with students—establishing an after-school girls' writing club and piloting an all-boys English class—helped her change her
identity and envision herself as a teacher *and* a leader.

Like Reilley, Anna Gilgoff, a high school English teacher, reluctantly
identified as a leader. However, as a veteran teacher, she had fully internalized

her teaching identity: "Teaching is my lifeblood," she wrote. Participating in her Writing Project site's 1997 Summer Invitational Institute and then facilitating Writing Project workshops started to shift Gilgoff's sense of herself.

> I had been a classroom teacher for over 20 years, but I'd honed my skills and grown my confidence as a teacher-consultant under the auspices of the Writing Project. I had grappled with the fear of facing my peers in workshops. I had spoken about writing practices and rubrics, standards and journals. . . . Unwittingly I had become a teacher-leader of sorts.

Gilgoff credited these experiences with giving her the courage to apply to the American Councils for International Exchange and participate in their teacher exchange program in the Republic of Georgia in October 2005. As an exchange teacher, Gilgoff played a leadership role by sharing how she teaches writing with the Georgian teachers. Once there, her strong identity as a teacher facilitated her work. Both teachers and students responded positively to the innovative, student-centered practices that she modeled. Despite this, Gilgoff's emerging leadership identity remained fragile. Gilgoff closed her vignette by saying, "[E]ven now, I'm still a little reluctant to think of myself as a leader."

Like that of Reilley, Gilgoff's vignette illustrates how identities develop slowly over time as one's expertise develops. Gilgoff's successful experiences in teaching teachers in her own community helped her believe that she had the capacity to contribute to change internationally. In turn, participating in the teacher exchange facilitated the process of seeing herself as a leader. For both teachers, engaging in successful practice as teachers and as leaders supported the development of a sense of agency. Reilley's and Gilgoff's stories not only show how identity develops over time but also illustrate how the writers came to see themselves both as teachers and as leaders within education.

Navigating Multiple Identities. The process of teachers moving from the classroom into formal leadership positions vividly illustrates how identities change over time. Such shifts also highlight Wenger's idea of multimembership, that is belonging to and identifying as a member of more than one community. In particular, these transitions show how individuals reconcile their dual identities as teachers and leaders—and the challenges that emerge. Two writers showed how they found ways to draw on their teaching knowledge in their formal leadership roles.

Scott Peterson (Chapter 4), who taught elementary school for over 25 years before becoming an elementary school curriculum director, described his reaction to his principal's invitation to apply for this district role.

> I told him I was deeply flattered by the offer, but I had been teaching so long that I had chalk dust in my veins, and this position was just too far removed from classroom teaching for my liking.

Here Peterson demonstrated his deeply held teacher identity while illustrating the administrator-teacher divide. Teachers and administrators engage in different activities, work with different people, and are therefore perceived to have different identities. Although Peterson rejected his principal's offer, he proposed a new district position to bridge the written curriculum and the daily life of the classroom. His vision relied on teachers' knowledge and expertise. Peterson's vignette illustrates how he worked to create a position that allowed him to maintain his identity as a teacher.

After 30 years of teaching high school, Linda Tatman, like Peterson, had developed a strong and positive identity as a classroom teacher. Her teaching identity was rooted in her ability to build a community with her students and engage them in inquiry. Following her retirement, she took a leap of faith and accepted a leadership role in her local Writing Project site's Masters of Arts in Teaching (MAT) program. This shift caused her to question her professional identity and her ability to work with teachers. Specifically, she wondered whether she would be able to contribute to teachers' growth as she had to her high school students' growth. She wrote, "Would I have anything new to offer?" She questioned how her expertise in teaching writing and building classroom community might help her face the challenges of her new role.

As Tatman began to work with the MAT teachers, she quickly learned that many of her teaching practices were directly applicable in her new setting: She got to know her students' strengths and struggles as teachers by asking questions; rather than telling them what to do, she offered recommendations and asked them to think about how they would adapt these ideas to meet their need; and she sought to build community online. As the MAT teachers embraced her recommendations and she experienced success, Tatman gained confidence in her work and, like Reilley, embraced her leadership identity. Further, Tatman actively designed and carried out her new role so that she could work collegially and collaboratively with the MAT teachers rather than hierarchically. By adapting her teaching practices to a new setting, she reconciled her teacher and assistant-director identities. Both Tatman and Peterson maintained their sense of themselves as teachers, balanced multiple identities, and defined who they were as leaders in relation to how others perceived them.

Developing Leadership Identities Socially

Identity is formed through interactions with others; it is not only developed internally (Lave & Wenger, 1991; Wenger, 1998). The literature emphasizes that cultural (c.f., Galindo, Aragon, & Underhill, 1996; Holland, et al., 1998) and role expectations (c.f., Cohen, 2008) help shape identity and practice. Here we show how these dynamics play out as individuals develop their identities as leaders.

Forming Identities Within Communities, Challenging Established Role Expectations. Changing positions within one's own school highlights how leadership identities get negotiated socially. Expectations of how individuals in well-defined roles behave shape interactions as well as identities. Yarda Leflet moved from serving as her high school's English department chair to working as its instructional assistant principal. Her vignette highlights how teachers immediately began to see her differently because of her new role and chronicles her efforts to transform the position. Leflet's conflicts with teachers stemmed from deeply institutionalized expectations about administrators: They do not understand teaching and therefore should not interfere in instructional matters, they work in a top-down way, and their requests ought to be treated as commands. These expectations caused internal conflict for Leflet, who both saw herself as a teacher and wanted to lead in a more collegial manner. To change how her teacher colleagues viewed and worked with her, Leflet acted in unexpected ways: She facilitated small-group professional conversations, not just professional development in stadium-style seating; and she asked questions and listened to teachers' responses before giving her own opinion. Spotlighting these practices, Leflet's vignette illustrates that while people's professional roles shape how others see and treat them, it is possible to change expectations and therefore transform the roles. To do so, individuals must recognize and address institutionalized expectations.

Confronting the Constraints of Enduring Social Categories. The level of power, status, and privilege assigned to, or withheld from, individuals and groups because of their race, gender, and social class represents another set of social factors that shape leadership identity. This is what Holland and her colleagues (1998) referred to as "positionality." A complete analysis of how social identities such as race, social class, gender, and language, as well as the complex intersections among them, shape leadership identity falls outside the scope of our research because we did not pose this as a central question. However, we view this as a key set of identity issues and, therefore, highlight examples from two vignettes.

Anna Gilgoff, who identifies as Italian American, reflected on the relationship between her cultural background, her gender, and her identity as a leader:

Before the Writing Project, I accepted "my place" in the world as one dictated by family obligation, cultural expectations, and geography.

Leaving the "neighborhood," let alone going to college, meant confronting fears and uncertainties. Where I come from, girls don't see themselves as leaders.

Here Gilgoff explored how early gender expectations contributed to her reluctance to identify herself as a leader. However, she noted, participating in the Writing Project and the teacher exchange program gave her concrete leadership opportunities and gradually prompted her to think differently about herself, setting aside the cultural and gender expectations about her role that she had grown up with.

Deidré Farmbry (Chapter 3), who identifies as African American, described her experiences confronting "race relations and educational inequity" as a regional superintendent in a large East Coast school district. Because of school district desegregation programs and changing neighborhood demographics, growing numbers of African American students were attending schools that had previously served Caucasian students. In her new administrative position, Farmbry immediately faced suspicion and overt hostility from White community activists "who disliked the fact that 'those kids' were invading their neighborhood," and pressure from the African American community to address inequities.

Farmbry decided to collect data to support her suspicion that African American students were not being well served. In two successive visits to the neighborhood high school, Farmbry observed two distinctly different schools—one mostly White, one mostly African American. She concluded, "In essence, the system of scheduling students resulted in the formation of racially segregated programs with noticeable differences in academic rigor and access to opportunities." The school's leadership team, composed primarily of Caucasian faculty and staff, challenged her observations and questioned whether they actually had a problem. This incident illustrated how the school reproduced typical social patterns around race and privilege and how the school's leaders invoked these in their questioning of Farmbry's analysis.

Farmbry's sense of herself as a leader, her position of authority within the school system, and her identification with the African American students and community pressed her to action. She did not accept longstanding community norms. She wrote, "So, on this journey, I developed the internal fortitude to use my position of leadership to steer a community in need of guidance in the right direction."

Collectively, these examples illustrate that leadership identity and practice are subject to widely held expectations about role and social status. At times, challenges to leadership identity emerge from external sources, as they did for Leflet and Farmbry; at others, struggles with identity are internal and arise from one's own history, as with Gilgoff. However, individuals do not have to conform to expectations. In order to change how others see them, individuals need to take action.

Taking Action, Making Change

Holland and colleagues characterized the ways in which individuals respond to social patterns and expectations as the "space of authoring." They elaborated, "The world must be answered—authorship is not a choice—but the form of the answer is not predetermined" (1998, p. 272). In the examples outlined above, each individual developed her or his identity as a leader in response to a set of preexisting social expectations and conditions. They also illustrated Holland and colleagues' point that individual responses are not predetermined and that individuals can engage in "improvisation" (p. 15). Reilley and Gilgoff showed that teachers can redefine leadership as collegial and learn to see themselves in a new way. Peterson, Tatman, and Leflet illustrated possibilities for redefining the typical role of administrators. Farmbry demonstrated that deeply embedded social patterns of racial inequities can be exposed and challenged. Such improvisations matter because they may create openings that lead to more widespread change.

When improvisations are encouraged in communities that sit on the edges of well-established social and cultural structures, they have the potential for making worlds—that is, for establishing new social and cultural patterns. Several vignette writers described how participating in communities that, like the Writing Project, operate differently from the formal school system supported them in developing a sense of their own agency to make change for themselves and others. Specifically, they adopted new practices aimed at building their students' and colleagues' sense of agency.

Elizabeth Davis, a veteran Washington, DC, teacher and "civil rights activist," described how she engaged her middle school students in working to save their school. Her vignette demonstrates Holland and colleagues' (1998) ideas: "space of authoring," the ability for individuals to improvise their own identities, and "making worlds," the ability to change social circumstances. Davis showed how she came to see herself as someone who could contribute to change through her own activism, her teaching, and her Writing Project involvement. And she demonstrated how she worked with her students to help them gain a similar belief about themselves. In this way, Davis improvised her own responses to the world and encouraged her students to do the same.

Similarly, Astra Cherry, now a retired teacher, recalled how conducting teacher research, through her master's program and the Writing Project, helped her "realize there was a chink in my teaching." Through careful study and collaboration with colleagues she learned that she could change her own teaching and work more effectively with her students. She facilitated teacher research groups so that other teachers could "discover the process of inquiry and the empowering effect it has on what they do in their classrooms." She described working with teachers who initially believed they must follow district mandates to the letter, even if these don't work for their students. Through asking questions, collecting and analyzing data, and talking with peers, these teachers, like Cherry, "feel empowered to question mandates and be a part of change." Both Davis's and Cherry's vignettes, as well as the other vignettes mentioned in this section, define leadership as collaborating and building the others' capacity to take action. Across the vignettes, the writers described forms of leadership that do not conform to widely held ideas about leadership. These leaders work to create opportunities and communities that challenge the status quo.

SUMMARY

Teachers develop their identities as leaders over time as they accept both formal and informal opportunities to lead. Although they gradually adopt other identities (leader, assistant principal, district curriculum coordinator), almost all maintain a strong sense of themselves as teachers. Thus, teaching identity and experience serve as resources for these individuals in their new roles, even when they face conflicts and rejection. They negotiate their identities and roles as leaders through their daily interactions with other teachers, students, supervisors, and those whom they lead. In such negotiations, virtually all these individuals attempted to shift what leadership meant— usually seeking to establish more collegial relationships, affirm other teachers' expertise, and accomplish positive outcomes for their students.

In transforming their leadership roles, they confronted and challenged widely held conceptions of what teachers, administrators, and leaders ought to be and do. Indeed, many vignette writers initially resisted labeling themselves as leaders because they did not fit the widely held definitions of leaders (i.e., hierarchical; decision-makers with formal titles). These writers show how participating in communities like the Writing Project helps them to define themselves and the very notion of leadership differently. Specifically, they seek to support others' learning, development, and action.

Chapter 2

Learning to Build Collegiality and Community

> Real leadership is "Let's talk about this idea. Let's develop some ways that we can implement this idea. What are your thoughts? Where do you see this going? and then, Let's move together in the direction that we have to go." And that's what really changes your school or your system or your state . . . when you have that shared responsibility for leadership. (Teacher, June 2006)

It has been over 25 years since Judith Warren Little (1982) wrote a classic work on collegiality, which demonstrated how teachers working together could lead to successful schools. Since then researchers and practitioners have developed a robust picture of what professional learning communities look like inside schools, how they develop, and how teachers and students benefit when they work well. The most recent scholarship examines how communities inside schools connect with the rest of the world to share expertise by looking at student work, developing performance assessments, and using data to analyze where students need help. Along the way, researchers have documented the challenges, risks, and limitations of collegiality and community.

In this chapter we take up the question, How do teacher-leaders learn to build professional collaboration in their workplaces? We begin with a selective history of research about collaboration and community in schools. This scholarship highlights the skills and dispositions leaders need in order to create community. We then present three vignettes that demonstrate teacher-leaders' perspectives on building community.

The research literature does not, however, show us how leaders—including teacher-leaders—develop the capacity to develop professional collaboration. Therefore, we turn to Lieberman and Wood's (2003) study of the National Writing Project, which names a set of "social practices" used by the Writing Project to build community, improve the teaching of writing, and support teachers' development as leaders (p. 21). We use these social practices, along with selected research, as a framework for analyzing how teachers' participation in a professional learning community *outside* school develops their capacity to create collaboration *inside* their workplaces. Our analysis, which draws examples from the three vignettes as well as others in the collection, concludes this chapter.

CREATING COLLEGIALITY AND COMMUNITY IN SCHOOLS: RESEARCH HIGHLIGHTS

Showing the Promise and Challenges of Collegiality

Little's (1982) foundational study of schools successful and unsuccessful in implementing continuous professional development began to teach us *up close* what teachers and principals do when they build collegiality into the culture of the school. Little focused on the day-to-day activities and structures that add up to real change in the culture of schools, such as building a shared language, planning and designing materials together, teaching each other, and observing one another. The means of expression were different then, but the successful schools, we would say today, are those that have built a collaborative learning community. Little's study emphasized the importance of:

- the *range* of professional development activities;
- the *frequency* with which teachers worked together;
- the selection of a *focus* for teachers' work;
- *reciprocity*, the amount of effort put forth by faculty; and
- *inclusivity*, the proportion of the faculty who participated in activities together.

In sum, Little's foundational study posited that a collegial culture facilitated effective professional development for teachers.

Several years later, Little (1986), critiquing her own work, which she felt had too enthusiastically embraced collegiality, wrote about the dilemmas and challenges in creating a collaborative community. In addition to the structural features she had identified earlier, she found that professional development is most influential when it includes an adequate and shared investment, thoughtful development, and a fair test of ideas. And teachers need to be involved in both the initial training *and* the implementation of new ideas. She noted that even when professional development creates collegiality, it may fail to change practice because it is too slick, modeling isn't made explicit, and practicality gets in the way of deeper change. Foreshadowing later criticisms, she noted that imposed professional development limits true collaboration and that school-based learning opportunities may threaten teachers' self esteem and professional standing.

Connecting Leadership With Building Collegiality

Lieberman, Saxl, and Miles (1988) subsequently documented the role of teacher-leaders working in three school improvement programs in New

York City. They uncovered a whole set of skills and abilities that link teacher leadership with the building of a professional learning community. Most important, the teacher-leaders who ran the programs first had to learn how to build *trust* and *rapport* with teachers. Sometimes this required providing support for teachers by getting them the materials that they needed; at other times it meant engaging in open and supportive conversation; while sometimes it involved modeling a new teaching strategy. But it became clear that building productive working relationships with teachers was the foundation for building collegiality and community in the school. In sum, building collegiality established the foundation for a different kind of leadership and different relationships among the faculty.

Identifying Different Forms of Learning Communities

Collegiality soon became one dimension of a larger set of practices now labeled *professional learning communities*. In these, authentic colleagueship grows when teachers work together over time, and when they change the way they work to fit students' needs. McLaughlin and Talbert (2001) conducted the first in-depth study on these communities, describing what they are, their characteristics, and the differences among them. They studied 16 high schools in California and Michigan during the early 1990s.

Principals, they found, set the stage for the kinds of communities that developed by the types of relationships they established with teachers, the way they allocated resources, and the nature of the support provided. Regardless of principals' roles, subject matter departments created very different norms and expectations for community, characterized by distinct ways of talking about students, content, and pedagogy. The researchers found three different types of communities: *weak, strong-traditional*, and *strong-innovative*. In these different communities, teachers either "enacted tradition" by teaching subjects as they always had without taking students' needs into consideration, "lowered standards and expectations" by watering down the curriculum and assuming that students were incapable of doing rigorous work, or "innovated to engage students" by creating new curriculum and teaching strategies that connected students' knowledge productively to school (p. 19). Teachers' differing commitments and approaches resulted in differing levels of student engagement and learning. Communities, McLaughlin and Talbert taught us, can either support the status quo or foster innovation and change.

Creating a Theory of Community Development

These early studies looked at collegiality and professional community in natural settings. While they pointed to key roles played by principals and teacher-leaders in developing and sustaining communities, they offered little information about *how* learning communities and colleagueship get created *from the beginning*. Grossman, Wineburg, and Woolworth (2001) published a study about how they tried to create a learning community by inviting the social studies and English departments of a Seattle high school to form a book club. In this way, they hypothesized, the teachers would learn from one another.

Grossman and her colleagues (2001) documented the community's stages of development as they facilitated, observed, and listened to the heated discussions about common books of the two groups. In so doing, they provided a set of conceptual hooks to understand the dynamics of moving from teachers' individual concerns to the formation of a learning community—including the inevitable conflicts that arise along the way.

The first set of conceptual hooks they provide characterizes the *stages of development* (Beginning, Evolving, and Mature) within a professional community. In the *beginning* of a developing community, people act as individuals. They do not see themselves as part of a group and, therefore, they ignore and suppress potential conflicts. As a community *evolves*, group members increasingly recognize the contributions of other group members. Conflicts start to be public and the group begins to discuss norms for group behavior. When a group grows into *maturity* people begin to identify with the group and take responsibility for each other. Members recognize that multiple perspectives are critical.

Grossman and her colleagues also identified four themes that cut across these stages that help us understand the inevitable tensions that arise for those developing and participating in a professional community:

- The "formation of group identity" (p. 988) involves establishing group norms and a collective sense of responsibility. Individuals become productive group members by casting off their sense of individuality and learning to engage respectfully with the group.
- "Navigating fault lines" (p. 988) shows how a group's stance toward conflict and differences changes as a professional community develops. Members initially deny differences in perspective and expertise and suppress conflict. As a group matures, members learn to capitalize on differences and use conflict productively.
- "Negotiating the essential tension" (p. 988) describes how a group comes to recognize that teacher and student learning are fundamentally intertwined.
- "Taking communal responsibility for individual growth" (p. 988) speaks to the development of a shared belief that teachers' responsibilities are to students. As the group develops and its work deepens, members establish a commitment to their colleague's growth

and realize that they have obligations to each other as members of a community.

Grossman and her colleagues' study teaches us how communities develop and what it takes in terms of both relationship and knowledge-building to create an authentic professional learning community.

Leading Community Development, Making Connections Outside

McLaughlin and Talbert (2006) analyzed several case studies drawn from different reform efforts, and help us understand the strategies employed by a variety of players to build community. They emphasized the importance of identifying a coordinator whose roles include "organizing the community's work" and "establishing an effective learning environment" (p. 40). Schools that succeeded in changing their culture had such leadership provided by either insiders or outsiders.

McLaughlin and Talbert also highlight the potential for a symbiotic relationship between teachers' professional learning *inside* and *outside* schools. They suggest,

> Teacher communities that stay within the walls of their school, like teachers who close the classroom door to colleagues, shut out the knowledge resources and collegial support essential to learning and change. Insulation from broader professional networks will stymie the improvement efforts of even the most engaged collaborative community. (McLaughlin & Talbert, 2006, p. 64)

Drawing on a case study of a middle school's involvement with the New York City Math Project (NYCMP), they show how teachers' participation in high-quality, off-site professional development coupled with facilitation from an on-site teacher-consultant allowed them to gain new conceptual understandings of mathematics, participate in a learning community, and engage in collective problem-solving about their teaching both inside and outside school.

Forming Professional Communities Around the World

Stoll and Louis (2007) collected cases of professional learning communities around the world, showing the power and the practices in different contexts. These case studies focus on new forms of organizing across role and subject area as well as across schools. For example, in the United Kingdom, teachers in different schools organized learning communities across schools to work on a particular subject area such as math or literacy, while in the Netherlands teachers formed communities in lieu of having formalized professional development.

These networked communities frame their work by *starting where the adult learners are* and rooting early discussions in going public with their practice. In all these learning communities, teachers' initial conversations focused on sharing a lesson or strategy with their colleagues and unpacking what did and did not work. This practice, we learn, serves to dignify the work of teachers and opens them up to their peers and to receiving knowledge from others (Lieberman, 2007). Echoing earlier research, Stoll and Louis also document the major impediments to the formation of communities, including lack of time, teachers being treated as objects for improvement, quick fixes of all kinds, and leadership unsupportive of structures for collaboration.

Critiquing Collegiality and Community

Over the years we have learned that neither collegiality nor community offers a magic bullet for changing the culture of teaching and learning in schools. In 2003, Hargreaves wrote about the problems that arise when collaboration meets up with hierarchical controls, referring to schools where administrators mandate that teachers work together. In such instances he observed a form of "contrived collegiality" (p. 165). Imposing too many requirements and restrictions on colleagueship from above hinders the relationships and shared work that aid teachers in learning from each other and building authentic colleagueship.

As professional learning communities became a popular reform tool, Hargreaves (2008) again weighed in with a cogent critique of communities worldwide. A number of the communities he studied had become "communities of containment," which, like earlier forms of contrived collegiality, were mandated from above (p. 177). Some, dubbed "performance training sects," imposed highly prescriptive curricular programs (p. 179). Others built "systems of surveillance" by engaging teachers in narrow, test-focused data analysis instead of the careful and deep consideration of a range of evidence about teaching and student learning envisioned by advocates (p. 181). Some simply remained short-term projects that failed to go deep and allow for challenging work.

Implications of Professional Learning Community Literature for Leadership

Research about collegiality and community over the past 3 decades highlights the potential benefits of professional learning communities: they provide opportunities for teacher learning and problem solving, support teachers in better understanding their students' interests and needs, and improve student learning (Lee & Smith, 1996). This research also reveals the risks of mandating professional community, where the "community" becomes a vehicle for implementing institutional scripts, for contrived collegiality, or for superficial engagement. Creating authentic communities, thus, is a complex matter. Leaders need to know how to:

- build collegial relationships with teachers;
- attend to the stages of a community's development;
- deal with the inevitable conflicts that arise;
- access and integrate external professional development resources; and
- overcome structural barriers to forming community.

BUILDING PROFESSIONAL COMMUNITY: TEACHER-LEADERS' VOICES

The research highlighted above has popularized collegiality and professional learning communities as school reform, but knowledge about how these ideas work in practice fills out the story. By reflecting on their own roles as community facilitators and leaders, the vignette authors make real what it means to develop community. The vignettes further demonstrate how these teacher-leaders developed the capacity to create learning communities, an idea not well developed in the research literature. The three vignettes included below highlight teacher-leaders' perspectives on forming professional learning communities in their workplaces as well as on their own growth as leaders.

Ronni Tobman Michelen, *an assistant principal, demonstrated the roles that formal leaders play in building professional learning community, including creating physical spaces for collaboration, facilitating professional conversation, and finding ways to highlight teachers' excellent work. Michelen's high school serves approximately 600 students, 97% of whom identify as being Dominican, in grades 9–12.*

My Daily Life

Ronni Tobman Michelen

WEDNESDAY, PERIOD THREE, ROOM 108: WEEKLY ENGLISH TEAM MEETING

It seems I always have three voices (maybe more) in my head as I plan for our weekly English team meeting. One is the voice of assistant principal, one of the teacher, and the other is my Writing Project voice. The three have sometimes learned to work together as collaborators. But it is the struggle, the tension, the questions the voices raise independently, the conversations they have among each other that excite me, stress me, and move the work forward.

My experiences with the Writing Project have taught me about working alongside teachers, facilitating, mentoring, celebrating, learning from mistakes, questioning, raising issues, sharing practice, recognizing the power of reading and writing, and treating teachers as professionals. How I work with teachers is the way I want teachers to work with students. I use the Writing Project model of sitting in the circle, teacher talk, sharing practice. It is the culture of the Writing Project that I bring to my English team meetings.

LINCOLN HEIGHTS HIGH SCHOOL, MARCH 1999: LEADERSHIP SHIFTS

I had been working in Lincoln Heights High School (a pseudonym), a large comprehensive high school, for 3 years as a teacher-consultant with the New York City Writing Project, when I was invited to take on the leadership of the English department. Over 75% of the teachers, along with the principal and the assistant principal of English, participated in after-school Writing Project courses or workshops that I facilitated. The work of the Writing Project was pivotal in removing the school from the "school under review" list that marks a school for closure if it does not improve attendance, grades, and Regents exam scores. I knew that when many teachers thought of the "assistant principal," they imagined totalitarian governments, Stalin, and military officers with black boots and condescending orders. This was a leadership opportunity for me to possibly shift the paradigm of what it means to be an assistant principal, and an opportunity to use Writing Project culture to chart the territory.

BACK TO THE MEETING

They wanted us to look but we had looked already
And seen the shaded lawn, the wagon, the postman.
We had seen the dog, walked, watered and fed the animal,
and now it was time to discover the infinite, clicking
permutations of the alphabet's small and capital letters.
Alphabetical ourselves in the rows of classroom desks,
we were forgetting how to look, learning how to read.
(Billy Collins, 1999, *First Reader*)

We sit in a circle like the Writing Project has taught me. I begin with a poem by Billy Collins about reading. I ask the teachers to take a moment to write about a success with reading they had this past week. We share and then write about a challenge. I am careful not to comment but allow the teacher voices to emerge. We take a deeper look at what defines a success and how a challenge can help us construct instruction. I ask the teachers to bring independent reading journals of two students to our next meeting. I remind myself to ask two teachers to facilitate with me at our next meeting. Our small acts are symbolic.

ROOM 114: THE ROADBLOCK

Room 114 is divided into two small rooms. The inner space was designated as my office and the outer space was to be used as a teachers' workplace. Thought was put into the design and into keeping me in the same space as the teachers. We furnished it with a long table and a round table, a coffee pot, refrigerator, and microwave. I wanted to enter conversations and present a less hierarchical, more organic form of leadership. Room 114 symbolically represented "leader as alongside person" and gave me an opportunity to bring my Writing Project leadership style to my new position. But my good intentions slowly unraveled.

Over the course of the year, my vision of collegiality and collaboration did not transform this workspace. Because I had a telephone in my office, teachers felt free to use it, which was fine at first. But soon my telephone became public, and several times I waited to sit at my desk until a teacher finished her conversation. In Room 114, the physical proximity seemed to separate the teachers and me. I invited teachers to share my space, but in doing so I did not consider their needs—a place to unwind, socialize, talk with colleagues about things other than school, eat lunch, and use a phone.

I wanted to lead as a coach, a friend. I wanted to nurture teachers and create a collaborative space among departments. But now there was tension and conflict. I was not comfortable walking into my own office. I had hoped Room 114 would be a place where teachers could share student work and look for ways to help students grow as readers and writers. Though sometimes this did occur, there were moments when this spirit was not part of the room. I felt hurt and angry, yet at the same time I recognized that I had to re-examine my role as assistant principal and the leadership style I had assumed would work. Something went wrong here and I wondered about the message I was communicating about my role and how I was being perceived. Time to get on the balcony and figure things out.

The teachers and I had different needs from this space and I realized that Room 114 was not going to build the alongside relationships I expected. I needed to look through the teachers' lens and see what they needed during their teaching day. I also needed to be honest with myself about my needs and how much I was willing to compromise. Our needs were different and it was my role to respect this. Another lesson learned, as I took on the role of assistant principal.

Assistant principal represents a position from which people expect formal authority, expect decisions to be made even though the act of making a decision can bring resistance. What happened in Room 114 was a case of a boundary crossed, and I knew I had to reclaim my space and my position as leader. But how could I do this without compromising my beliefs about working with teachers and moving the work forward? People want leadership, and being a leader can mean offering direction, expertise, and support. But I realized I was getting too close, and the space between my assistant principal self and my teachers needed a boundary. Come September I would take the old dean's office in the back of the school. The space would offer me privacy and a way to collaborate on new territory. This incident made me a stronger leader. I've come to learn that every move and decision I make is symbolic of my values and beliefs.

CELEBRATIONS

With administrative work, observations, and other duties of assistant principal, I had forgotten about the joy of celebrating student work, and I decided I would organize an event. I posted flyers advertising our poetry slam and highlighted that prizes would be awarded. I invited teachers to encourage students and collect poems they would like to submit, but I placed no pressure on teachers to participate. I scheduled the poetry reading for period three when I knew all the English teachers were free. Twenty-five students read their work and every English teacher was present. We clapped, we cried, we laughed. We left the room a team connected by the joy of why we teach.

PROFESSIONAL DEVELOPMENT DAY: JUNE 2006

It is professional development day and I have hired the American Place Theatre Literature to Life program to present a workshop based on *The Things They Carried* by Tim O'Brien (1998) to both English and social studies teachers. Room 115 was set up like a theatre and for 3 hours we worked together around the issue of war and using drama to teach. I purposely selected Room 115 because both teachers have made this classroom feel like a home. The walls are covered with student work, and a visitor can examine the academic journeys students took this year by examining the classroom walls. As we reflected on the power of this workshop, one teacher commented on a character map, a poster showing an understanding of a character's journey through a novel, which students had composed based on their reading of *Sula* by Toni Morrison (1973). "Let's each save a piece of work and start our new school year with a best practice presentation like we did with the Writing Project." I knew we had a way to begin our September 2006 semester and the idea did not come from me.

I am coming to think of assistant principal as conductor, responsible for each musician successfully playing her part, allowing solos, encouraging individuals to shine, practicing and rehearsing and revisiting and revising until we get it right; responsible for following the music but placing one's own individuality into it, and thereby producing a harmonious sound that brings joy and reflection to our audience. Perhaps that's what the job is. To be a leader, but to know that after so many rehearsals the orchestra can perform without you. The refrain of the three voices chants the chorus I have been raised with: "Teachers teaching teachers." This is the mantra that connects the three voices and builds my capacity for leadership and keeps me comfortable in my skin.

Kim Larson, *a state curriculum administrator, drew on her Writing Project experiences to build a professional learning community in an unlikely place—among her colleagues at the Nebraska State Department of Education. Her vignette demonstrates how teacher-leaders call on similar sets of skills when creating learning communities in any setting.*

THREADS OF UNDERSTANDING

Kim Larson

- The best teachers of writing are writers themselves.
- Teachers provide the best instruction for other teachers.
- Anyone, no matter her ability level, can improve her writing in a supportive context with other practicing writers.
- True school reform comes through democratic partnerships across grade levels.
- Teachers, students, and communities benefit when teachers form networks with other teachers and draw on collective expertise.

(Belief Statements, Nebraska Writing Project)

I remember sitting among a circle of teachers during the first Summer Institute I attended, listening as Robert Brooke, the Nebraska Writing Project's (NWP) longtime director, said that teachers are the best teachers of other teachers. I was intrigued, but hardly believed it was true. I was sure that someone outside of my school had all of the answers to my questions about learning—why some children could grasp concepts easily, and others struggled to make sense of the very same ideas. I thought that knowledge could be passed from these experts to me. In much the same way, I was also sure that knowledge was transmitted by *good* teachers to their students, easily and efficiently. But because of my involvement with the Nebraska Writing Project over many years, I now understand that learning anything is a process—that knowledge isn't transmitted from one to another, but is developed within oneself over time through interaction, support, trust, need, interest, and opportunity.

When I began my job as reading and writing director with the Nebraska Department of Education (NDE), I knew that teachers are the best people to make the decisions that can positively impact students' learning—not people far removed from that environment in state and federal institutions. I also knew that change doesn't happen as a result of mandates, but rather through individual self-discovery and collective collaboration.

As a teacher of beginning readers and writers, I had felt valued, respected, and successful—but I lacked the same confidence in my new role as the interpreter and disseminator of information about state literacy education requirements. If I was going to succeed at leading state literacy initiatives, I would need to find ways to hold onto my long-held beliefs about teaching and learning and utilize them as I met new expectations and responsibilities. My understanding of the complexity of teaching and learning would be the thread that would bind my many job responsibilities.

SEAMS THAT CONNECT AT NEBRASKA DEPARTMENT OF EDUCATION

After I had been 2 years on the job, my supervisor asked if I would like to organize learning teams for our curriculum department to learn together about incorporating reading as a tool for learning into all content areas. She knew that my participation in learning teams through the Nebraska Writing Project had truly changed the way I thought about teaching and learning. I thought about one of these groups—one whose members implemented after-school writing clubs for first- and second-grade students. We read, wrote, and studied learning together for many years as we provided young writers with a special time for writing outside of the regular school day. This study team, supported by the Spencer Foundation, had provided me with support, time, and focus for learning about the conditions and environments that encourage developing readers and writers.

At first it was hard to imagine that there might be people at NDE who would be interested in participating in ongoing study teams. Normally the work that we do does not involve deep study of topics—time is too taken up by the day-to-day assignments that hover and circle endlessly. But I happily agreed to colead the project, knowing that our studying reading instruction together could impact the work of teachers in many content areas and grade levels across Nebraska. We presented this unusual chance for learning, opening the invitation to join learning teams to all staff, not just our curriculum team. I was thrilled when over 40 department staff volunteered to participate, agreeing to read and discuss Rachel Billmeyer's (2004) *Strategic Reading in the Content Areas* in groups of four to six over the course of a semester.

Our group, like the NWP groups, met monthly. We represented diverse perspectives—reading/writing, career education, marketing, world language, and early childhood, and even our NDE commissioner joined us for some of the meetings. Together we established our own reading schedule, deciding to read a chapter or two each month. I selected Billmeyer's book because it provides a structure for learning team study, with suggestions for prereading activities and after-reading discussion ideas that teams could utilize to aid their own understanding. The book focuses on why supporting all students as readers is critical, and offers strategies that could be used in any classroom. I was pleasantly surprised when group members arrived at our meetings with smiles, eager to talk about what we were reading, writing, and thinking. We looked forward to this time together—time that was relaxed and filled with comfortable, open conversation. Our meetings seemed to be a refreshing change of pace.

As we learned about reading instruction, we engaged in the same activities that could benefit students' comprehension of text in classrooms, thus discovering, through personal experience, the value of supporting students as readers. Many staff incorporated what they learned from their group's study into workshops they presented, teaching teachers of business, agriculture, social sciences, world languages, and others the strategies that could support their students as readers.

Like my experience with the Writing Project study team, this project provided people at the department with a chance to learn together through ongoing interaction. It gave us a chance to get to know others whom we would otherwise just pass in the hall on the way to a meeting or the elevator. We could learn about them personally as well as about their work. We continue to learn through reading book clubs, which are now a part of the learning culture at NDE.

CONNECTING ALL THE PIECES

People often ask me if I like working for a state department of education. I sometimes surprise myself when I answer *yes*. Although there are endless meetings, assignments I'd rather say a polite "no thank you" to, and never enough time to get everything finished in a day, I am glad for the opportunities my job brings. I am able to influence policy, learn with and from people with diverse perspectives, and often guide an assignment so that it takes on my philosophy— the guiding principles of the Nebraska Writing Project. And every once in a while I find a way to create a learning opportunity for others that resembles the many I experienced during my years with the Writing Project.

I know I will continue to make a difference in the world of education through the learning environments I create for others. I'll continue this work even though the impact of the moments I share with others in our office and across the state may sometimes remain unknown to me. What I like most about my job is that I have discovered how to connect what I learned through my work with the Nebraska Writing Project with my work as a state curriculum director. I no longer exist between two separate worlds.

Paul Epstein, *an elementary school reading specialist, described how he collaborated with other teachers in his school to improve the teaching of writing and begin to build a professional learning community in his school. Epstein's elementary school, located just 2 miles from the downtown of a midsized city, serves approximately 350 students in preschool through fifth grade. Of the students, 70% are eligible to receive free and reduced-price lunch; 90% are Caucasian, 9% are African American, and 1% are either Asian American or Hispanic. In his vignette, Epstein also reflected on how serving as a leader in his Writing Project site helped him build community and teacher leadership in his school.*

THE COURAGE TO LEAD: CREATING A PROFESSIONAL LEARNING COMMUNITY AT MY ELEMENTARY SCHOOL

Paul Epstein

It's one thing to stand up in front of strangers and to ask teachers to try something they may not have tried, to show them ways to teach writing; if they don't buy it, you may never know. You won't pass them in the hall, you won't see them at lunchtime, you won't sit in faculty meetings with them. And you won't be too concerned what they think of you.

It's quite another thing to get up in front of your coworkers and tell them they should be teaching differently.

During the first 7 years of my Writing Project involvement, being a teacher-leader was something I practiced outside my own building. Inside I maintained a low profile. I had done a couple of one-shot workshops and invariably felt uncomfortable. This kind of inservice would not likely have a genuine impact, but I could not envision another way. But in 2001 my thinking changed. I took responsibility for the success of a new Writing Project site I had helped create, the Central West Virginia Writing Project. If I could not be a leader in my own building then I could not in good conscience ask others to step into leadership roles in theirs.

At that time, my school's scores on the fourth grade state writing assessment were very low. No other teachers in my school felt confident about teaching writing, and writing was not part of the school improvement plan. I proposed to our principal that we share the responsibility for teaching writing among all the grade levels, starting with collaboratively setting benchmarks for our students in writing. What would we expect of students by the end of the year? As each grade level came to a consensus, many teachers expressed their anxiety—they agreed most students should be able to reach the benchmark, but they weren't sure how to get them there.

That year I also started a new job as a Title I reading teacher; I would hold classes in a new computer lab, integrating reading and technology. Among other things, I wanted to use the computers to write and publish with students. So I started a quarterly schoolwide anthology of student writing, determined to include every student before year's end.

Looking for ideas and feeling pressure to meet our benchmarks, a couple of the teachers came to me for suggestions. I found it satisfying to offer advice, though I didn't have easy answers. Two first-grade teachers asked me how they could get their students to write in complete sentences. I'd seen many demonstration lessons by primary teachers during Writing Project Summer Institutes and knew that students would develop these skills only after much practice writing freely. I encouraged the teachers not to instruct the students to write *sentences* at first, but to tell them to write *stories* instead. I advised them to hold off on making corrections until after the students finished writing; I explained that students would revise and edit in the publishing stage. Slowly they began experiencing some success. I became a mentor in teaching writing to a few other teachers as well, informally asking about their progress and offering suggestions. Teachers often wanted to show me the results. I enjoyed reading the students' stories and encouraged the teachers to post them in the hallway and show them to the principal. I also worked harder at recruiting teachers for the Summer Institute, and got three teachers to apply and attend.

EXPERIENCING SUCCESS, EXPANDING THE WRITING PROJECT BASE

My school began to see itself and be seen as a school that was strong in writing. Writing lined the hallways throughout the building, interspersed with art. Every 9 weeks when we published our student anthology I sent home personalized invitations to an authors' reception. Many parents came or sent cookies. I invited school board members and county administrators and sent them copies of the anthologies. Our writing scores rose.

In 2005, Melinda (a pseudonym), a fourth-grade teacher, participated in the Writing Project Summer Institute. She had demonstrated a willingness to take on leadership by volunteering to lead the faculty senate her first year in our building. She had come from a much smaller school that was closed and consolidated into ours in 2003. Melinda had been the librarian there, but now she was teaching fourth grade, the level of the annual statewide writing assessment.

DEEPENING THE WORK AT MY SCHOOL

For a couple years, I had been interested in implementing Writing Project–sponsored school-based study groups. In the model I proposed for the 2005–2006 school year, the Writing Project would pay the study group leader and contribute $250 for books and supplies. Our principal had Title I funds to pay the teachers to stay after school.

This would be the 3rd year that my school had study groups. Unfortunately, our study group meetings that were supposed to last 2 hours lasted 1 hour and 1 minute, teachers habitually showed up late, and discussions were often superficial or off-topic. Though some learning took place and new strategies were tried, a "professional learning community" had not been created.

I planned to recruit one of the Writing Project teacher-consultants in our building to lead the new study group. I would attend as a participant, collaborate with the leader, but try my best not to intervene. I wanted the leader to experience leadership without interference. I decided to ask Melinda. I was concerned about asking her because although she had done good work during the Summer Institute and came back enthused, she expressed insecurity about her abilities as a classroom teacher, even though writing scores had improved during her first year teaching fourth grade. I worried it would be like a baseball coach bringing a player up to the majors too soon. What if the study group was a disaster? What if the teachers resented her? Would she shy away from leadership or Writing Project work in the future?

One early question I had for Melinda was "How are we going to get teachers to take this seriously and stay for 2 hours at each meeting?" Her answer assured me that she would be a capable leader. "This is important," she said, "and I'll just tell them up front, either commit to spending the time or don't show up." In fact, two dropped out after the first meeting.

SUPPORTING LEADERSHIP, DEVELOPING A PROFESSIONAL LEARNING COMMUNITY

Melinda started each session with a prompt designed to either take teachers away from their daily grind or get them to reflect more deeply on their work. She made mini-presentations about her classroom successes and encouraged others to do the same. At our first meeting, one teacher expressed her absolute lack of understanding about teaching writing by asking something like, "How can you ask students to write essays when they can't even write a complete sentence? Don't you have to teach English skills first?" Melinda spent a good deal of time trying to answer; I sat having an internal dialog about whether and how to intervene. A skeptical teacher could keep the group from moving forward. After awhile I steered the conversation back to Melinda's plan, which included reading an excerpt from *Because Writing Matters*, a National Writing Project (2003) publication that clearly explains best practice in teaching writing.

The study group met each month from November through March. Melinda and I were considered study group coleaders by the group, and we fell into an easy collaboration. At times she and others would turn to me to answer tough questions or give advice because I clearly had more knowledge and experience. But I also tossed the ball back for group discussion and always turned to Melinda for an okay. Sometimes I felt Melinda was doing too much talking and not sharing leadership and responsibility with the group as much as she should, but I did not intervene. I did meet with her informally before or after school to praise her work, telling her what I thought went well, asking what she thought, and discussing what she was planning next.

All the teachers were positive in their evaluations of the experience. Melinda was good about allowing each teacher to express her anxieties about teaching writing and getting the rest of us to help her answer the teacher's questions, veering away from other plans she may have had. The study group came much closer to my vision of a professional learning community than previous study groups in our school, even though scheduling was difficult, and not all teachers attended each meeting.

REFLECTING ON THE IMPORTANCE OF OVERCOMING FEAR OF PEERS

Melinda proved a good choice as a teacher suited for leadership. Having me as a coleader helped her overcome her anxiety about leading peers. She articulated the goals of the National Writing Project clearly and explained why increasing the amount and quality of student writing would enhance critical thinking, thus improving scores on statewide reading and math tests as well as the fourth-grade writing assessment. Now, not only are there other Writing Project teachers in the building who "get" the importance of writing, but there is another mentor to whom teachers may go for ideas and advice.

Since I overcame my reservations about being a teacher-leader in my own school, our school climate toward writing has changed. Nearly half of the classroom teachers are Writing Project trained. Our current principal is supportive of our efforts. And teachers who are hesitant to teach writing get encouragement from those with more experience. These changes took place over 5 years spurred by my efforts in teacher-to-teacher collaboration. I feel lucky to be in a position in which I have contact with all the classroom teachers and can be a resource for them. Having completely gotten over any fear of offering advice to colleagues, I can encourage others to share freely. Diminishing such fears is key to creating a professional learning community.

DEVELOPING THE CAPACITY TO CREATE PROFESSIONAL
COMMUNITY: OUR ANALYSIS

In addition to providing leaders' firsthand accounts, the vignettes teach us how these teacher-leaders developed the knowledge and skills to create professional collaboration and community. To frame our analysis of how the vignette authors gained this capacity, we turn to Lieberman and Wood's (2003) study of two National Writing Project sites. The authors identified a set of social practices that convey NWP's norms and purposes through the Summer Invitational Institute. These social practices include (p. 22):

- approaching each colleague as a potentially valuable contributor;
- honoring teacher knowledge;
- creating public forums for sharing;
- turning ownership of learning over to the learners;
- situating human learning in practice and relationships;
- providing multiple entry points into the community;
- guiding reflection on teaching through reflection on learning;
- sharing leadership;
- promoting an inquiry stance; and
- encouraging a reconceptualization of professional identity and linking it to community.

Writing Project teachers come to understand that learning in a community helps them frame problems and figure out together how to solve them. Below we identify how the vignette writers subtly draw on the Writing Project's social practices as they build collaboration and community in their workplaces. We include examples from the three vignettes included in this chapter as well as other vignettes not included in this chapter.

Creating Forums for Shared Learning

Learning together is central to both the joint work of professional learning communities and the Writing Project's Invitational Institute. Across the vignettes, the writers figured out how to organize and create the conditions for honoring teachers' knowledge and, at the same time, brought people together to learn new approaches with their peers. As they formed new communities, they brought the power of working together that they experienced in the Writing Project into their daily work.

Christy James (Chapter 3), a social studies master teacher, convinced her middle school colleagues that they needed to do more reading and writing with their students. At weekly meetings, she modeled one strategy at a time, based on "the teachers' responses to monthly writing prompts, my classroom visits, and their curiosity." In this way, she began to *turn ownership of learning over* to her peers, who gradually began to seek her out for additional suggestions. She *honored her colleagues' knowledge* by setting aside time for everyone to share samples of student work and for grade level teams to adapt the week's strategy to meet their needs. Finally, she included personal writing and designed the meetings so teachers would experience the strategies they would teach. This *grounded their reflection on teaching in their own learning.* James's efforts were effective; the teachers slowly incorporated writing strategies into their social studies repertoires.

When teachers moved out of the classroom into administrative roles, they continued drawing on the social practices to build professional communities. Ronni Michelen, who worked full time for her Writing Project site prior to becoming an administrator, believed that creating a community in which teachers helped each other improve the teaching of reading and writing represented one of her central roles as a high school assistant principal. As she worked with the English department, she developed a professional learning community by engaging teachers in reading and writing together. Specifically, she invited teachers to write about and share their successes and their challenges without her comments. This allowed the group to develop a shared definition of success and to help each other address their teaching challenges.

In a single activity, Michelen embedded four Writing Project social practices:

1. honoring teacher knowledge
2. creating a public forum for sharing
3. viewing each member as a valuable contributor
4. turning ownership of learning over to the learners

Over time, the teachers appeared to internalize these practices, with one teacher recommending that all of her colleagues save a piece of work to share with each other at a future meeting. Michelen's vignette illustrates not only that she learned to build community through her Writing Project experience but also that the social practices work together to create professional learning.

Addressing Educational Problems Collaboratively

Several vignette writers showed how publicly acknowledging teaching problems and work challenges can serve as a foundation for collaborative learning. They formed communities both inside and outside their schools and work places. Some examples showed how communities help individual educators solve problems of practice, while others illustrated how educators work collaboratively to address an overarching concern.

With 1 day each week to work with her peers, Cec Carmack, a fourth-grade teacher, set out to involve her whole school in raising scores on the state's fourth-grade writing assessment. To start the conversation, she asked all the teachers to bring anonymous class sets of writing to their grade team meetings. Carmack describes the second-grade team's efforts to analyze the writing's strengths and weaknesses together. Although teachers initially viewed sharing their students' work as risky, as the meeting progressed "anxious energy dissipated into serious considerations over each piece of writing." After teachers finished jotting notes about "elements of effective writing and trends in mistakes," Carmack charted teachers' ideas about students' writing strengths. This approach *promoted an inquiry stance*, and Carmack reflected, "They came away with a different kind of knowing about their students' writing." Their new understanding encouraged the second grade teachers to *take ownership of their learning* and begin to plan strategies for engaging their young writers.

Similarly, Kim Larson worked to develop a professional learning community among state department of education staff members as they learned about "incorporating reading as a tool for learning in all content areas." Based on her experience with the Nebraska Writing Project, Larson structured learning teams so that they had *shared ownership of learning*. Specifically, they made decisions about what to read, how to facilitate their conversations, and when to meet. At the same time each group read a common text and "engaged in the same activities that could benefit students' comprehension of text." These study group activities gave staff members a "personal experience" with the strategies that they would teach teachers and also allowed staff members to learn about each other personally and professionally. In this way, Larson *situated human learning in practice and relationships*. The learning teams supported staff in learning new professional development and teaching strategies and simultaneously fostered a "learning culture" at the state department of education.

Building Community by Developing Leadership in Others

Creating a sense of communal responsibility for individual learning is one of the literature's central ideas about developing and sustaining professional communities. One way in which the Writing Project develops such a sense in the Summer Institute is through *sharing leadership*. From the vignettes, we learn how the writers nurtured others into leadership roles in order to *create public forums for teacher sharing, dialogue, and critique*.

Paul Epstein, a Title I reading teacher and codirector of his Writing Project site, decided to provide leadership around writing in his school using what he learned through the Writing Project. He quickly realized that one of his tasks was to *develop leadership* among other teachers. After a couple of years his school was starting to "be seen as a school that was strong in writing." He wanted to create a stronger sense of community, however, and decided to start a study group. When he launched the group, he engaged and supported another Writing Project teacher as his coleader. As they worked together and his coleader grew, teachers gained "another mentor in the building . . . to go to for advice." Thus, as he nurtured his colleague's leadership skills, Epstein simultaneously facilitated the growth of professional community in his school.

Developing teacher leadership is central to the core mission of the Writing Project. Although this process begins in the Invitational Institute, it can't end there, or a Writing Project site's ongoing community weakens. Karen Smith's site faced just this situation and learned that it would lose its funding unless it built more teacher leadership capacity. As a member of the leadership team, Smith suggested that they invite teacher-consultants who had participated in the Invitational Institute during the previous 5 years to a "return institute" to "rethink" the site's work. Smith pushed for an open-ended agenda that would draw on participants' knowledge and "allow the teacher-consultants to feel a stronger role in creating the institute." Here she enacted the social practices of *approaching each individual as a potentially valuable contributor* and *honoring teacher knowledge*. Although this design made some participants uncomfortable, it allowed participants "to see themselves as a core component of the [site's] teacher leadership structure" (*sharing leadership*). Following the institute, Smith identified, supported, and encouraged a new group of leaders who "stepped out and took risks," helped revitalize the site, and began to *reconceptualize their professional identities*.

SUMMARY

Together, these examples illustrate how the vignette writers internalized and enacted some of the Writing Project's social practices as they worked to create new professional communities in their schools, districts, and Writing Project sites. Along the way, they encountered the challenges and rewards of leading professional learning communities. The communities that they built seemed to avoid some potential pitfalls noted by researchers; in particular, the authors did not describe situations in which contrived collegiality emerged, or the scripted implementation of mandated curricula. The vignettes contribute to our understanding of how teachers learn to lead by demonstrating how the authors enacted approaches to building community that they learned and internalized through their participation in the Writing Project. This suggests that professional development and social networks can foster teachers' leadership capacity through modeling and reflecting on desired practices.

Chapter 3

Learning to Make Conflict Productive

> An understanding of conflict within community is crucial to practitioners', reformers', and researchers' understanding of how such communities form, cope, and are sustained over time. Conflict can create the context for learning. (Achinstein, 2002, p. 422)

Teacher-leaders face seemingly ubiquitous conflict, especially when they attempt to make change or build professional communities. Educational conflicts arise from many sources: differing values and methods of teaching; race, gender, and class differences; different grade levels and subject matter orientations; and differences in status (e.g., new versus long-term teachers, administrators versus teachers, district versus school). Because conflict can pit people's ideas against each other, cause interpersonal difficulties, and challenge long-held assumptions, people learn to develop the appearance of well-being and working together (Achinstein, 2002; Grossman, Wineburg, & Woolworth, 2001; Hargreaves, 2003). In light of these challenges, it is easy to see why teachers and those in formal leadership positions develop many ways of avoiding conflict.

Despite the risks, experience both within and outside education suggests that productive conflict represents an important source of learning and change (Achinstein, 2002; Deutsch, 2006; Grossman, Wineburg, & Woolworth, 2001). So how can educational leaders use conflict to create a different way of addressing the many complex problems of school and classroom practice? How do we think about conflict? What do we know that might help us see conflict as a source of learning to be resolved productively? We summarize several theoretical perspectives from the conflict and conflict resolution literature that are directly relevant to teachers when they assume leadership. We present three vignettes that explore how teacher-leaders confronted conflict. Drawing examples from these vignettes as well as others, we conclude by examining the kinds of conflicts that educational leaders, including the vignette authors, face, and we show how their vignettes illustrate their approaches to learning from and resolving conflict.

THEORIES OF CONFLICT AND CONFLICT RESOLUTION

Beliefs About Change and Conflict

There is a great deal of evidence that people hold implicit theories about people's abilities to change. Dweck and Ehrlinger (2006) described *entity* and *incremental* as critical theories for understanding conflict. Those who hold entity theories about people's ability to change believe that people have fixed traits and see individuals "as embodiments of a group(s) stereotypes" (p. 320). Such individuals make rigid judgments about others, act defensive about their own beliefs, and may use labels to dismiss or dehumanize others. In contrast, those who espouse incremental theories seem less likely to stereotype and are open to negotiation and education. Interestingly, they are not very open to evidence that says that some people will not change. They may be more than willing to accept the fact that people are trying to change, but are disappointed when others do not actually open up for improvement.

Our implicit theories about people's abilities to change may contribute to conflict by causing us to make assumptions about people that may or may not be true. These theories matter for teacher-leaders because they call attention to the complex and different ways that people respond to change and give clues about how to approach conflict.

Power and Conflict

Power theorists try to find the sources and effects of power in conflict situations. Although there is an extensive literature offering a wide array of explanations of how power and conflict relate, the most useful theory for our purposes was developed by McClelland (1975). He described a developmental framework for categorizing people's experiences and expressions of power. Initially, people obtain assistance from others by offering *support* and creating a dependence relationship, which can be benign, oppressive, abusive, or controlling. When individuals gain *autonomy*, they have enough power so they don't need to depend on anyone else. *Assertion* refers to having "power over" others and using this power to get someone to do something that might otherwise not have been done. *Togetherness* allows people to have "power with" others and work with a sense of a collective effort.

McClelland argued that problems arise when people get fixated on their own ideas (such as stereotypes) or approaches to power and when their views do not fit the realities of a situation. Many teacher-leaders find themselves seeking togetherness, but find that the situation, context, and role expectations may push them to adopt different power orientations to resolve conflicts. For example, teachers often expect to be told what to do because of typical bureaucratic norms in schools. Several teacher-leaders in our study worked hard to figure out how to respond to these expectations and define *some* boundaries and frameworks, while still encouraging teachers to take agency and greater control over their work.

Environmental Factors

Coleman (2006) described how intergroup conflicts, deeply rooted in historical contexts, continue to shape social interactions. He viewed people as agents embedded in a structure of history. Because of this, people sometimes accept inequities in a culture and feel more powerful or less so based on their social positions. Cultural myths get perpetuated that support hierarchical relationships or dominant superiority of a particular group. Such factors fuel conflict and lead people to believe that circumstances can't be changed. Teacher-leaders must be cognizant of the environmental factors that shape others' perceptions about students and about role expectations as they work to address conflict.

A Social Justice Perspective on Conflict and Mediation

A number of researchers are developing new theory and practices for mediating conflict with an explicit social justice orientation (Wijeyesinghe & Jackson, 2001). They question several underlying assumptions of conflict resolution theory: that conflicts arise primarily from individual differences, that mediators ought to remain neutral, and that conflicts can be resolved by developing a mutually accepted plan. While social justice mediators, like other conflict resolution theorists, emphasize "empowerment and democratic participation" (Wing & Rifkin, 2001, p. 183), they also organize for value-driven change. Specifically, such mediators actively engage organizations and groups in gaining a deeper understanding of how race and social justice connect, and they take these factors into consideration when working to resolve conflicts. Wing and Rifkin noted, for example, that membership in particular social groups—including those delineated by race, gender, and social class—puts people in different power positions, influences the nature of the conflict, and needs to be taken into consideration during conflict resolution. Therefore, when mediators take a neutral stance (a typical practice), they gain an insufficient understanding of the conflict and may be unable to address the underlying dynamics fueling the conflict.

Wing and Rifkin argue that in order to both resolve microlevel conflicts *and* advance social justice, mediators need to develop their own understanding of oppression and social identity development and gain the skills to facilitate discussions of how these dynamics impact conflicts. In particular, such theorists are working to understand how using racial identity and oppression theories can change the way conflicts get explored and resolved in

our increasingly diverse society. These theorists argue that traditional methods of resolving conflict cannot, and should not, ignore the presence of race
and oppression as the underlying sources of many conflicts. Because many
people find explicitly addressing race to be difficult, social justice theorists
are developing strategies for bringing race productively into both the discussion and resolution of conflict.

Productive Conflict

During the 1940s, Morton Deutsch and his research group began to formu-
late a way of theorizing about cooperation and competition (Deutsch, 2006).
Their work provides the foundation for the now vast literature on conflict
resolution. Their beginning idea was that conflict could be a productive way
to learn. And the group went to work doing research on the different kinds
of conflicts and how they could be resolved with a positive outcome. They
examined and described the conditions that foster cooperation:

> Cooperation is induced by similarity in beliefs and attitudes; readiness to be
> helpful; openness in communication; trusting and friendly attitudes; sensitivity
> to common interests; de-emphasis of opposing interests; and finally orientation
> toward enhancing mutual power. (Deutsch, 2006, p. 31)

In the process, they quickly realized that most people learn through their life
experience how to engage in, or more than likely ignore, situations where
they are involved in conflict.

Deutsch and his colleagues (2006) were especially interested in how
building cooperative conditions could ameliorate the negative effects of
conflict—knowledge relevant for any leader or change agent. When leaders are trying to change a system, key people must support the change, but
alone this is not enough. Leaders must educate themselves and members
of the group(s) involved in order to create a win/win situation. Those involved in change processes must understand what is going to be expected
of them, and they need to accept and embrace the changes. When inevitable conflicts arise during change processes, leaders sometimes need to
reframe the conflict so that all involved view it as a mutual problem to be
resolved through collaborative effort. Finally, building norms of cooperation is critical to resolving conflict productively. A leader does this by empowering others to contribute to the common good, placing disagreements
in perspective by identifying common interests, and trying to understand
others' perspectives.

Deutsch (2006) identified three skill areas that leaders need in order to
manage the conflicts that arise when people are learning new ideas or forming new relationships. He argues that leaders need to be skillful in building

rapport, engaging in conflict resolution, and creating positive group processes. To *build rapport*, leaders can learn to help reduce fears and tensions, establish a framework for civil discourse, and foster realistic hope. In the process of doing these things, leaders help group members overcome their resistance to moves that the leaders make.

Leaders can learn a range of *conflict resolution skills*, either intuitively or from others. These skills, which are at the heart of managing conflict and making it productive, include the following:

- Identifying the conflict openly,
- Making the issue a *mutual* problem,
- Listening actively and being responsive,
- Acknowledging others' needs,
- Encouraging and enhancing others,
- Putting oneself in another's shoes,
- Identifying shared interests, and
- Dealing openly with difficult people.

(Deutsch, 2006, p. 38)

Finally, Deutsch teaches us that to make conflict productive, it is essential that leaders internalize the norms of cooperation and then build them into *positive group processes*. He mentions four such norms:

- Constantly looking for common ground amidst a conflict;
- Building on the ideas of others;
- Taking responsibility when there are harmful consequences and being willing to ameliorate the situation; and
- Emphasizing the positive and working for the possibilities of constructing resolution of the conflict.

(2006, p. 35)

Although these lists of skills and norms look simple and even obvious, leaders need to internalize them because they are critical to getting work accomplished and building win/win situations. Further, as Deutsch warns us, in the heat of conflict, it is important for leaders to recognize their own "hot buttons" so that they can control their own emotions and continue to model norms of cooperation.

The knowledge, skills, and processes needed to build cooperation and turn conflict into a learning situation, which Deutsch and his colleagues describe in general terms, are broadly applicable in education. In the 1980s and 1990s, for example, conflict resolution programs involving peer and teacher mediators flourished in education (Morton, 1991). Deutsch's recommendations also appear critical to developing professional communities and making deep changes inside schools.

LEARNING TO HANDLE CONFLICT: TEACHER-LEADERS' VOICES

While the theoretical explanations about conflict provide useful frames for analyzing the sources of conflict, the literature and practice of *conflict resolution*, including those approaches with a social justice perspective, provide important tools for making conflict public and learning from it. The vignettes that follow illustrate a variety of conflict situations, one left unresolved and two others that are resolved productively.

Mimi Dyer, *a new high school English department chair, encountered resistance from teachers when she unilaterally implemented a series of curricular reforms. Reflecting on her experience, Dyer viewed this work as a "failure," but learned valuable lessons about working collaboratively with teachers in order to resolve philosophical conflicts. The 2,200 students in Dyer's suburban high school are 66% Caucasian, 18% African American, 9% Hispanic, 4% Asian, and 3% multiracial. The school, which achieves Adequate Yearly Progress annually, has received national recognition for its Advanced Placement and character education programs and its positive school culture.*

BUILDING COMMUNITY: IT'S PERSONAL

Mimi Dyer

Sitting in the parking lot and looking at the huge expanse of blue roof covering the building, I wonder if I am the right person for the job. Our school was built to alleviate overcrowding, so most of the staff not only know each other but seem to be ingrained in the *this is the way we do things here* attitude. According to my principal, I have been selected as English department chair because I am not indoctrinated into the district's long-established views of English education. "You have fresh ideas that we need; I'm hoping you can help move us forward." Gosh, I hope so too, I thought, but I'm not so sure. Maybe I should stay in the classroom where I'm happy and confident that I make a difference in children's lives.

Nonetheless, I'm thrilled for the opportunity to lead a new department at a new school, and I can't wait to see the excitement of "my" teachers when I introduce them to National Writing Project concepts: collaboration, writer's workshops, community research, writing as performance, thematic approaches, authentic writing, and electronic portfolios. How wonderful!

Unfortunately, some vocal veteran teachers, steeped in tradition that values *desk-in-rows, speak when spoken to, and the teacher has all the answers* pedagogy, did not find those ideas so wonderful. They wanted no part of change, especially introduced by someone they perceived to be an outsider. During that 1st year, I made three major curricular decisions. Based on research that U.S. students need more exposure to world cultures, I adjusted the sequence of courses to include world literature. I discarded the traditional 10-word-a-week, stand-alone vocabulary study that had been in use forever in favor of a teacher-developed, 18-week cumulative plan based on frequently used SAT words. I also asked all students to keep electronic portfolios, including reflections. Suffice to say, there was a lot of talk about me in pairs and small groups.

During the 2nd year, with the district's support, I ended the requirement that students write a traditional literary analysis research paper; instead, teachers had the option of engaging students in community research, which involves primary research. The teachers did not like the changes that had been instituted nor the direction that I was leading them. So, in response, the teachers began an e-mail campaign to building and district administrators requesting my replacement. It was clear that I was faced with an adversary I couldn't defend against, and while I was supported at the building and district levels, they could not very well dismiss a whole department in favor of a single person. So when a new position opened at the school, I jumped at it, but in my heart I knew I had failed.

Needing help, I turned to those around me for advice: my father, an extraordinary military and professional leader; and my NWP site director. At first they commiserated with me, but they would not allow me to feel sorry for myself for long. Through long conversations, they helped me put the situation into perspective and see how I could use the experience to my advantage. My father related stories from World War II about the value of retreating in the face of overwhelming odds to regroup and change tactics. My site director enlightened me with how she had handled challenges such as mine in her own career. Finally, I began to see the possibility of using the defeat as a learning tool for reinventing myself as a leader.

Knowing that knowledge is power, I returned to graduate school in leadership and, at the same time, assumed the role of codirector of an initiative at my NWP site funded by the National Endowment for the Humanities. I also began a new job at my school as instructional lead teacher, charged with providing staff development for all staff members. So while I was learning the theories of good leadership, I was also able to put them into practice in my building and at my local site. During this time I also made careful observations of others' leadership qualities that more clearly defined the kind of leader I wanted to be.

Most important, I continued to ask myself the question, "What did I do in my successful classroom that I didn't do in my department, and how can I use that knowledge to my advantage?" The answer, I determined, was in establishing a classroom collaborative community reflective of the NWP model. My students spoke the same language, read together, wrote together, and shared together in a supportive, nurturing atmosphere where there were no inane comments and no unintelligent questions. Working individually and collectively to solve problems, we found comfort and security in the learning environment and became open to new concepts and challenges.

I came to the job believing that others would appreciate my success and follow my example. Instead, I learned that in any organization, especially one as traditionally entrenched as education, leaders must foster collaboration by promoting cooperative goals and trust with each teacher before trying to implement change. I did not handle my detractors well; instead of building a collegial environment I created an adversarial one in which the naysayers held court.

In my new position, tentatively at first, I began my leadership reinvention, and 3 years later I'm still working on it. Instead of focusing on what I might do wrong with the negative minority, I'm developing positive relationships with small interdisciplinary groups of teachers. Together we articulate our own personal values and create opportunities for improving student engagement through innovative curricular ideas and approaches. I meet with them one-on-one to develop short-term and long-term professional goals; and as a group we search for opportunities to change, grow, and improve while recognizing and celebrating the contributions made by individual successes.

In short, we are creating a professional learning community culture that values communication, shared values, collective vision, and an ability to understand that a profession is made up of individuals who have passions, hopes, dreams, and challenges. By establishing personal relationships—as I had with my students—we are able to challenge the status quo, knowing that support is only a step away. I've come to understand that failure is not necessarily a bad thing unless I don't learn from it, and I have rediscovered the excitement of collaborative teaching and learning.

Christy James, *a middle school master social studies teacher, confronted a district administrator about a new curriculum policy that dropped the district's emphasis on integrating literacy into social studies, and focused on test preparation. James illustrated that finding common ground and demonstrating good work can help resolve philosophical conflicts. James' middle school, located in a mostly rural district, serves roughly 900 students in grades six through eight. Of the students, 72% are eligible for free and reduced-price lunch, and demographically are 45% Caucasian, 40% African American, and 15% Hispanic.*

Rules Worth Breaking

Christy James

I sat in stunned silence, staring at our new district administrator as if he'd just sprouted five heads, and wondered if any of those heads knew anything about education or staff development. He had just announced a new policy to all the school-level master teachers at our December meeting. With 5 months left until testing, we would spend the remainder of our early-dismissal staff development days looking at assessment and student achievement on the state tests. The wide triumphant grins plastered across many of my colleagues' faces almost knocked me to the floor. The new mandate and my fellow master teachers' reactions didn't actually surprise me, but the reality of the situation stung. This loud band of naysayers had wanted an end to all "this touchy-feely literacy nonsense," and their wish had been granted. In the past, they had constantly questioned *why* we needed to incorporate reading and writing into social studies and had refused to share information with their teachers.

I knew reading and writing belonged in every classroom for every student every day. The problem wasn't my core beliefs. The problem was that I taught middle school social studies. And now, according to our new administrator, we didn't have time to spend on reading and writing in social studies.

Accepting the master teacher position in July had seemed like a perfect fit. I would provide staff development once a month to my department, focusing on incorporating literacy instruction in social studies. But what had once been my dream job turned into my worst nightmare after that meeting in December. Reading, writing, and thinking were supposed to be my focus, not standardized test scores. Research clearly showed the correlation between reading, writing, and students' testing success. If students could read and comprehend information, if they could write and explain their understandings, then they could definitely pick out the correct answer on a multiple choice test.

It wasn't just that I despised spending time on assessment or that my job description and focus had changed midstream. The naysayers of content area literacy had won. Worst of all, I felt I had lost credibility with my teachers. Everything I'd promoted tirelessly all first semester had just been thrown out the window.

Our department had made incredible strides with our instructional practices. Not all the social studies teachers in my department had come to our first meeting, or even our second and third meetings, ready to embrace the wonders of reading and writing. One teacher even brought a copy of his teaching certificate to show me he wasn't certified as a language arts teacher. I understood that reading and writing were uncharted territories. I also understood that students' troubles with reading and writing caused some of teachers' biggest frustrations.

I wet the teachers' feet without throwing them to the sharks. I began with a best-practice framework to establish the research basis and impact of including reading and writing every day. Initially, I made my point using statistics; I knew the numbers would grab their attention. They were awed by the sheer volume of reading we require of students in social studies, and the amount and variety of writing students complete before leaving high school. Once I sensed everyone could see the potential value of increased literacy to help students learn and succeed, I began to share strategies and activities through examples of my students' work and their learning reflections. I felt it was vital that I lead by example to demonstrate my commitment as well as the success students could achieve.

Our learning and implementation model was simple. Based on the teachers' responses to monthly writing prompts, my classroom visits, and their curiosity about ideas related to the strategies we learned, I chose a focus for each of our meetings: using poems for two voices to compare and contrast historical events and leaders; writing letters to explain historical perspectives; having students pass notes back and forth as interactive responses to reading; and describing how artwork reflected the values of different cultures. During each meeting, I explained and modeled just one strategy related to our topic. At the end of the meeting, I asked teachers from each grade level to plan together ways to incorporate the new strategy multiple times in the coming weeks. At the beginning of the next meeting, I set aside time for our department to share student examples and stories of what had worked and what the students had struggled with when using the most recent activity.

Every staff development session seemed to be an awakening for at least one teacher, and always for me. During our meetings we actually experienced and practiced the reading or writing strategy being highlighted. We started each session with a quickwrite, a short timed writing to generate ideas and focus thinking, sometimes about our students or sometimes about issues in education, like homework or even testing. I explained to my department that I was using their quickwrites to gauge their classroom needs and to plan my visits and staff developments; they could use the same idea in their classrooms as a barometer of their students' understanding of content. By October, the eighth-grade teachers decided that quickwrites were more beneficial than daily geography questions at the start of class.

With each passing meeting there were more nods of agreement, more questions about activity specifics, and more classroom success stories. Around October, the teachers began to realize that these strategies were quickly embraced by students, had an impact on learning, and allowed teachers to easily assess students' grasp of the material. I stressed that all the strategies fit naturally with what they were teaching and helped prepare students for the state tests.

After the testing news, I reflected on where we'd been in August and where we were in December. Our literacy learning model really had been working—beautifully. I was confident that the integrated reading and writing instruction my department was now providing was better for test scores than anything I could share with them about assessment from the district office. I just couldn't stop our learning now, yet that was exactly what I was being told to do, with testing invading our staff development. It became clear to me that rather than explaining the district's waffling to my teachers, I would demonstrate my teachers' transformation to the district. Ending our literacy focus simply wasn't an option. It was a good thing I'd never been very good at following rules.

I knew that someone from the district office would be sitting in on one of my staff development meetings. I decided on a proactive approach. I mentioned that our school was having problems with the testing focus and that we'd like to continue with our content literacy development. The administrator didn't understand at first, and explained that he was giving me all the testing information and materials at our master teacher meetings. In a series of e-mails and one unpleasant phone call I explained how completely invested the teachers were in bringing reading and writing into our social studies classrooms. In the end, I put myself and my teachers on the line, "Why don't you come see for yourself what we're doing before the next meeting?" It was important for him to see firsthand what teachers were accomplishing and how students were responding.

Needless to say, I had not won a new friend, but to the administrator's credit he did come to our school. He observed my class for two periods and surprised the teachers by peeking into seven other classrooms before the meeting. He sat in the back of my classroom in his white button-down shirt and conservative navy tie, common attire for district administrators in my region, peering at nearby tables to see what students were writing. I sensed that he might be expecting a dog and pony show; what he encountered was reading and writing seamlessly integrated into social studies instruction. He participated in our meeting and even wrote part of a circular story designed to help students sequence historic events. He meticulously took notes as teachers discussed their recent attempts and adaptations, and showed student examples using last month's ideas on using poetry as a write-to-learn strategy. The teachers couldn't contain their enthusiasm and inundated the administrator with classroom examples and unsolicited literacy-filled testimonials. As he left that day he simply stated, "You seem to know your teachers' and students' needs. Carry on. Testing can wait." I smiled at the victory. The test wouldn't wait; like the administrator, we were all under pressure to raise test scores. I knew it wouldn't be a problem because the students were learning to comprehend what they read and show they understood through writing.

My department lingered after the administrator left, celebrating what they understood of the day's success. They knew they'd impressed him with their knowledge and passion. What they didn't know, and didn't need to know, was that they'd just saved themselves from a few more months of testing hell and probably had saved my job. Their learning reminded me that sometimes rules are meant to be broken.

Deidré R. Farmbry, *who served as a high school principal and as a regional superintendent in a large urban school system, described how she confronted disquieting evidence about student learning and achievement. Her vignette illustrates strategies for productively addressing conflicts rooted in racial inequities. When she served as a principal, her high school served a student body of whom 99% were African American and roughly 85% received free or reduced-price lunch. As a regional superintendent, she oversaw nine schools, elementary through high school, in an area of the city that was confronting demographic changes.*

LEADERSHIFT: DETOURS, DEAD ENDS, AND DESTINATIONS ALONG THE LEADERSHIP JOURNEY

Deidré R. Farmbry

I hate getting lost! Thank goodness for Mapquest, advanced navigation systems, astute traveling companions, and landmarks. Although we rarely set out to get lost, most of us frequently find ourselves in unfamiliar territories searching for a route to get back on track. Embarking on a journey of educational leadership very often results in getting lost somewhere along the way. From the point of entry to the point of departure, the traveler encounters detours and dead ends never referenced on roadmaps received in leadership preparation courses, creating the need to discover new paths. In order for the traveler to survive, leadership in education calls for constant reassessment and reorientation of where one is in order to revise the route for getting to where one ultimately hopes to be.

DESTINATION: THE PRINCIPALSHIP

I taught for 15 years at a high school with a 99.9% African American student population. After a 5-year hiatus, during which I worked in a supportive capacity to a superintendent, I was ultimately appointed as principal of this high school. I felt very confident returning to the school, believing that my knowledge of both people and place would enable me to rise to the expectations outlined for me by those who had decided to send me "home." I felt no need for a roadmap, for I knew where I was going—or so I thought!

Instead of stepping into the context I expected, I stepped into a situation where teacher morale had declined, serious student behavioral infractions had escalated, and academic expectations for students had plummeted. The first indication of the extent to which the landscape had shifted came in the form of a teacher's comment during an informal focus group. All she said was, "Make me feel safe, and I'll do whatever you want." While other teachers brought me up-to-date on the development of small learning communities, the desperation reflected in that one teacher's statement shifted my thinking from what I *wanted* to do, to what I might *need* to do instead.

Given her statement, not only did I, as a leader, have to revisit and redefine what I had the *will* to do, but I also had to grapple with what I had the *skill* to do. Did I have the capacity to make this teacher, or any other staff member, feel safe? What was needed beyond currently existing resources? How would I balance the expectation that the principal provide a safe climate with my personal belief that safe environments hinge on collective responsibility and ownership? Faced with that one request—"Make me feel safe"—I went from traveling down a familiar road to the state of being lost! I needed help in overcoming this roadblock.

So I did what lost travelers do—I asked for guidance, and in the process I developed my skill in garnering resources and developing partnerships. The two most helpful traveling partners were a prominent sociologist and a probation officer. Drawing comparisons between the streets and school hallways, the sociologist helped staff improve their ability to navigate shared space respectfully with students perceived to be threatening. He conducted study groups with parents, teachers, and 12th-grade students, all of whom read his book describing the consequences of fear when people glance at each other suspiciously and then retreat into safety zones of anonymity, never taking the time to get to know each other.

By helping the three study groups understand that positive relationships begin when people step into each others' worlds and foster understanding through communication, the sociologist empowered participating staff and students to take the lead in alleviating tension in the school culture. He also assisted parents in developing a new framework for their involvement at the high school level. The probation officer, meanwhile, placed at the school due to my persistence in appealing to city officials working in the juvenile justice system, provided some assurance for wary staff that the most troubled youth were under his observation while at school.

In the course of making it through this detour of focusing on student behavior rather than student learning, I had to address issues of race, perceptions, and stereotypes—topics not discussed in my leadership preparation classes. I had to seek perspective before making critical decisions about how to allocate resources, including my own energy, to address this issue of teachers' fear, lest it become all-consuming. I had to balance my belief that most students were intent on doing the right thing with the perspective of many staff members who were convinced that the school was under siege by a handful of students intent on causing disruptions to the learning environment. Although I was committed to being a leader at my home school, I was not committed to remaining lost on the issue of discipline—an issue that too often derails a focus on student achievement in urban settings. So I was quite proud of the stance I took, enabling me to eventually get back on the road where I wanted to be.

DESTINATION: REGIONAL SUPERINTENDENT

My next leadership position presented yet another circuitous route. After serving 3 successful years as a principal of a high school, I became a regional superintendent in a blue collar, predominantly Caucasian section of the city, characterized by schools that were becoming increasingly minority each year, much to the outrage of many community residents who disliked the fact that "those kids" were invading their neighborhood. Most of the schools' racial diversity resulted from African American students who chose these schools as part of the districtwide busing program for the purpose of desegregation, or from low-income African American students who lived in two subsidized housing developments on the fringes of the neighborhood.

When I was appointed to be in charge of the nine schools in this section of town, I was greeted with a high degree of suspicion regarding my intentions and my allegiance. One neighborhood rebel made sure that there was some veiled reference to me in the community newspapers by writing articles for the gossip section questioning, "Why in the world is the principal of *that* school coming to lead here?" At this stage of my journey, my leadership transition plan had to focus on developing an understanding of the context, with a special emphasis on analyzing the overt hostility I was experiencing. I had to mentally process why I, as an African American female in a leadership position, might be viewed with suspicion and skepticism in a section of town still predominantly Caucasian. Dealing with personal attacks to my integrity was new for me, so here I was, once again, *lost*.

I found strength while traveling down this unfamiliar path from a spiritual guide, the Serenity Prayer: "God grant me the serenity to accept the things I cannot change, the courage to change the things I can, and the wisdom to know the difference." While the words helped me get a handle on the scope of need versus my personal capacity, I continued to feel the intense pressure of the African American community urging me to investigate and resolve some of their concerns—such as course placement and disciplinary imbalances that they attributed to racial prejudice—and the Caucasian community daring me to do so. In facing such polarized pressure, I sought to arm myself with evidence supporting my hunch that significant numbers of students were not being served well, and then to use that evidence to build a coalition willing to support me in implementing changes contrary to the way "things have always been done here."

And proof was not hard to find. I remember returning to my office after my first visit to the neighborhood high school and commenting that the school was still predominantly Caucasian. After my second visit the next day, I returned commenting that the school I had seen was predominantly African American. My two successive visits highlighted that the impression one gained was highly dependent upon the program viewed. Stark racial segregation was the norm inside the building, even though this school was listed as a site of the school district's desegregation plan, and was highly coveted by minority students beyond the community. In essence, the system of scheduling students resulted in the formation of racially segregated programs with noticeable differences in academic rigor and access to opportunities.

When I informed the principal's predominantly Caucasian cabinet of my two distinct snapshots, I was asked, "So do you think we have a problem here?" For a fleeting moment, I began questioning my own perspective, thinking that perhaps I was lost! Then it hit me that the leaders of the school were the ones who were truly lost in their understanding of the inequities that the school was perpetrating. From the tone with which the question was asked, I knew that the cabinet was trying to disarm me; I was making them vulnerable to the tension-laden fallout that occurs when raw racial realities are exposed. In the name of exercising responsible and responsive leadership, I was intent on unraveling the protective cocoon the leadership team had spun to their benefit and the benefit of *some* children.

Yes, the journey through the terrain of race relations and educational inequity got tougher. My curiosity fueled questions about course selection, retention rates, suspension statistics, grade point averages, honor roll status, extracurricular participation, and notification processes for postsecondary opportunities such as scholarships. The intentions of my questioning were viewed as having a double meaning because the color of my skin matched the complexion of the students for whom the data provided clear evidence that "the ways things have always been done here" were not benefitting all students equally. Despite periods of intense discomfort, I came to view this road not as a detour, but as a road I most definitely was destined to travel!

Having learned the value of "wise guides" on my previous detour, I took a similar route. I hired a very young Caucasian female who had just moved into this community to fill a key position on my leadership team. She assisted me with bridge-building by possessing the insider's eyes and ears at community meetings, sometimes accompanying me and at other times going as my representative.

I retained the services of a no-nonsense, "in-your-face" consultant on race relations who happened to be African American. She conducted cross-constituent workshops and was able to unearth deep-seated beliefs that hampered the capacity of the schools in my region to serve all students equitably.

I purchased Beverly Daniel Tatum's (1997) book *Why Are All the Black Kids Sitting Together in the Cafeteria?*, and dedicated a portion of time at my principals' meetings to reading and interpreting the book, focusing on its application to the school sites. The principals and I talked about jumping to conclusions, misreading situations, and letting our own biases obstruct rational thinking. The collaborative processing of the book's content, particularly the sections describing the connection between racial identity and group affiliation as they influence friendships and bonding, assisted the principals in gauging their responses and their interaction with staff members who persisted in assigning negative meaning to simply being human in diverse settings. The book promoted open dialogue about sensitive issues and contributed to our biweekly meetings becoming a safe place for touchy yet critical topics to be discussed.

Finally, I arranged for community meetings to be held in the housing project where some of the bused students resided. This change of meeting location helped in breaking down the feelings of alienation that had disenfranchised many African American parents.

What I gained by being a leader in this section of the city was an understanding of the power of schools to be the locus of change for community issues, and the responsibility of leaders to *coach* their constituents out of destructive comfort zones. I arrived at this destination, as I did at my previous one, expecting to be able to focus on teaching and learning. However, I realized that this journey had to begin, not with a focus on academics, but with a focus on attitudes.

I had to enhance my own capacity to navigate this road, so I read books pertaining more to sociology than education, for I needed material related to identity formation and how communities develop and protect themselves from the encroachment of "others." Here the "others" looked like me, so I felt compelled to develop a leadership agenda for change based on a moral imperative predicated on my belief that separate *is* unequal. I could not be one of those leaders who turned a blind eye to the bold contrasts I witnessed. So on this journey I developed the internal fortitude to use my position of leadership to steer a community in need of guidance in the right direction.

ON THE ROAD AGAIN!

Wherever I go, I take with me a trunk full of treasures amassed through my leadership journey—treasures I value as critical components of leadership. All of my treasures are indispensable, and all are worth sharing. Call on them to help you stay focused on the final destination while enjoying the lessons to be gleaned from those inevitable detours and deadends that strengthen you along the way. My constant traveling companions, always in my trunk, are inquisitiveness, open-mindedness, courage, sight and insight, candor, moral conviction, spirituality, strength, collaboration, determination, resiliency, and integrity. I acquired them through trials, yet they are the essence of the triumphs of leadership and the benefits of embarking on the journey!

MAKING CONFLICT PRODUCTIVE IN EDUCATION: OUR ANALYSIS

Conflict is part of our lives, both inside and outside education. Learning how to make conflict productive can help us figure out how to move educational reform forward. Research about professional community and educational leadership both shows the risks of not addressing conflicts, and highlights some examples of how conflict can be used in a positive way. Three themes tie together the vignettes and selected educational literature on conflict:

- Addressing conflicts that arise from role and status differences,
- Confronting conflicts related to differences in teaching values and practices, and
- Making conflict public in order to resolve it.

Addressing Role and Status Conflicts

In schools, well-established role expectations dictate the social rules and norms of behavior. For teacher-leaders, these factors help us understand why teachers resist both leadership from their peers and advice about teaching from administrators. In a study of distributed leadership, Hallett (2007) showed what happened when a new principal attempted to get a faculty that saw itself as successful to better serve their students and raise achievement. The principal quickly and unilaterally changed several organizational routines, all of which involved increasing her monitoring of curriculum and instruction, without first building relationships. The faculty mobilized against her, little change in instruction occurred, and test scores declined.

Cultural expectations for administrator-teacher relationships and the attendant conflicts are visible in the vignettes as well. Yarda Leflet (Chapter 1) moved from being a well-regarded English department chair to her school's assistant principal. Her vignette describes the conflicts that arose when her fellow teachers pushed her "out of the club," rejecting her instructional ideas and ignoring her presence. During her first year as an administrator, she drew on her expertise with building positive group processes to regain her effectiveness as a school leader. In particular, she listened actively to teachers' ideas, encouraged and enhanced their work, and built on others' ideas.

Confronting Conflicting Values and Teaching Practices

A central source of conflict in education, and one that often gets papered over, is differences among educators in their beliefs and practices. Grossman, Wineburg, and Woolworth (2001) found that one major challenge to forming an interdisciplinary professional community was getting teachers to discuss and learn from subject matter differences. Rather than exploring differences, the English and history teachers initially tried to develop the appearance of well-being and working together.

Similarly, Mimi Dyer, one vignette author, learned that she, as a new English department head in a suburban high school, could not simply mandate that her colleagues adopt innovative teaching strategies. Here the teachers, who relied on traditional teaching approaches, complained to administrators, forcing Dyer to apply for and accept a new job. In this instance, conflicts around philosophical and pedagogical differences were left unresolved. Through reflection on the situation, Dyer realized, "I did not handle my detractors well; instead of building a collegial environment, I created an adversarial one in which the naysayers held court." Through this "failure," Dyer realized that she could more productively resolve philosophical conflicts by "promoting cooperative goals and trust." Both Dyer's personal experience and Grossman and colleagues' (2001) research are consistent with Deutsch's (2006) conflict resolution theories; those involved needed to start by building trust. Although Dyer was unable to resolve the initial conflict productively, she learned from the experience and approached her new leadership role differently.

Conflicts in teaching approach exist not only among teachers in the same school, but also between policy makers and teachers. Christy James, a middle school social studies master teacher, described a conflict with the district as it shifted its focus from using reading and writing for learning social studies to preparing students for test-taking. She had already overcome potential conflict with her peers, who were developing important skills and whose students were demonstrating promising progress with their learning. With the district, James presented direct evidence that her approach was working successfully, thus demonstrating her shared interest in (if a different approach to) student learning with the district. Although James was not addressing a group conflict, her successful approach to addressing conflicting teaching philosophies reflects Deutsch's (2006) principle of emphasizing the positive, in this instance showcasing teachers' and students' good work.

Making Conflict Public

Sometimes making conflict productive involves identifying and addressing it openly (Deutsch, 2006). In her study of the role of conflict in professional communities, Achinstein (2002) contrasted two middle school faculties' stances toward conflict. Both schools rated high on measures of professional community and both espoused shared values. In one school, the faculty united around its belief that a group of "problem children" couldn't be reached; those teachers who voiced dissent and attempted to reframe the problem were silenced in public forums and ultimately left the school. Here, shared attitudes and cooperation left inequities unaddressed.

In contrast, the second faculty created a variety of public forums in which teachers could actively debate their ideological and professional differences. Such debate pushed them to try new approaches, which conflicted with some faculty members' educational beliefs, to better support their African American students' learning. While conflicts meant that faculty members sometimes felt uncomfortable, their overall shared values allowed them to confront differences productively. Achinstein's findings, compatible with Wing and Rifkin's (2001) frame for addressing conflict, also highlight how explicitly addressing race prompted deeper explorations of how to support all children's learning.

Similarly, Deidré R. Farmbry's vignette illustrates how putting conflict on the table was critical to changing educators' expectations for African American students' learning. First as a principal and then as a district superintendent, she selected partners to help her publicly "address issues of race, perceptions, and stereotypes." She also listened carefully to everyone's concerns and worked to reframe the problems so that she could engage faculties in confronting the "deep-seated beliefs that hampered [their] capacity . . . to serve all students equitably." In doing so, she illustrated how making conflict public can address entrenched environmental factors.

Farmbry relied both on classical conflict resolution techniques and on techniques that are guided by a social justice orientation. In both administrative roles, she sought to make problems of low and inequitable student achievement into both public and shared problems, as Deutsch (2006) suggests. At the same time, Farmbry did not simply maintain a neutral stance but explicitly addressed race (Wing & Rifkin, 2001) through common reading, data analysis, and facilitated conversation. To build cooperation among staff and community members, she sought out allies (a sociologist at the high school and a consultant on race relations in her region) to complement her own knowledge and skills.

SUMMARY

Conflict arises among individuals, groups, and countries and is a natural part of everyone's life. There are literally scores of theories about conflict and why it is so prevalent. We have suggested a few that help us understand the nature of conflict and how it relates to teachers as leaders. People have strong *beliefs*, and beliefs about conflict, which sometimes encourage stereotyping people and treating them accordingly. Sometimes people are open to change within certain boundaries. Interestingly, developmental theorists positing different phases of understanding power relationships end with a "power with" orientation, precisely where teacher-leaders start their work.

Sometimes *environmental* factors help perpetuate conflict, when conflicts arise out of historical myths that are accepted as truisms. In recent years, a group of social identity theorists have raised questions about the effects of race, gender, and class, as well as other social identities, on how conflicts are understood and mediated. Although in its infancy, this line of work advocates a social justice agenda and in so doing wrestles with how to mediate both macro and micro influences on conflict.

Among the teacher-leaders described in this book, conflicts arose in many different places and for different reasons. For some it was conflict over the different philosophies of district and teachers; for others it was the difficulty of moving from being a teacher to being an administrator; and for others it was addressing entrenched environmental factors. In each case, the leaders learned to go public with differences and forge collaborative programs.

Chapter 4

Reflecting on New and Old Knowledge to Learn from Practice

> In obstetrics . . . if a new strategy seemed worthwhile trying, doctors did not wait for research trials to tell them if it was all right. They just went ahead and tried it, then looked to see if results improved. . . . And that approach worked. (Gawande, 2007, p. 189)

Atul Gawande's (2002, 2007) perspectives on how surgeons learn echo a growing body of social science theory and research that articulates how adults learn to carry out their work and professional responsibilities. He writes persuasively about the complexities, mistakes, and individual situations that doctors confront in their daily work (2002). In addition, he explores the role of individual practitioners' diligence and ingenuity in making the field better (2007). Doctors, even surgeons, constantly learn from practice. Like doctors, teachers and teacher-leaders develop their practice as they confront challenges and experience successes in their daily work. In this chapter, we draw on selected literature, both within and outside education, to frame our analysis of how teacher-leaders learn from their own experiences and contribute to improving teaching and learning. This literature grapples with several common concerns: how formal, codified knowledge and day-to-day practice relate to each other; how people learn through doing; and how professionals play a role in creating knowledge and practice. Recent literature examines the role of communities in shaping peoples' initial learning as well their ongoing learning.

The vignettes illustrate these theories and help us understand how teachers learn to lead by examining and drawing on their own experiences. To illustrate how the vignette writers learn from practice, we include four complete vignettes in this chapter, as well as examples drawn from several additional vignettes.

RESEARCH AND THEORY ON LEARNING FROM PRACTICE

Reflective Practice

In 1983, Donald Schön, a social scientist and consultant, published his influential work *The Reflective Practitioner*. In it, he critiqued professional preparation and highlighted the growing divide between what gets taught in graduate professional programs and the real world of work: "[P]rofessional knowledge is mismatched to the changing character of the situations of practice" (p. 14).

Schön argued that identifying and solving problems that lack predetermined solutions represent core components of professional practice. Schön highlighted how professionals rely on "reflection-in-practice," or "a [professional's] reflective conversation with a unique and uncertain situation" (p. 130), in order to engage in problem solving. This iterative process, which happens virtually instantaneously and is often tacit even to the practitioner, involves the following practices:

- identifying the unique features of a situation, considering how it is similar to problems encountered in the past, and thereby turning it into a solvable problem;
- conducting experiments, which involves identifying and trying out potential solutions to the problem;
- discovering through these experiments which solutions work and which do not; and
- if necessary, conducting additional experiments until the practitioner finds a satisfying solution.

While Schön took into account the impact of organizational processes, his conceptualization of reflective practice remained largely individual rather than social.

Sociocultural Learning

Over the past 3 decades, organizational theorists and social scientists have gradually developed social theories of learning. For these scholars, like Schön, learning represents a central part of practice. Brown and Duguid (1996), for example, argue that "the composite concept of 'learning-in-working' best represents the fluid evolution of learning through practice" (p. 59). They show how ongoing learning unfolds when initial training and technical manuals do not reflect a job's complexity.

Based on ethnographic research about copier repair technicians, they identified three processes through which these individuals learned. Through *narration*, individuals created stories containing "accumulated wisdom" (p. 66) that ultimately allowed them to solve problems. Repair technicians often began repairs by talking to the users of the copier to find out its history, and they collected information from the machine itself. Sometimes the technicians worked with specialists to fully develop the story. Some stories got told and retold and, therefore, became a vehicle for technicians to share knowledge. Through *collaboration*, the copier repair technicians not only trade stories with each other but develop insights about what the problem might be and identify potential solutions. Finally, Brown and Duguid described the processes through which individuals build a "shared understanding" (p. 67) of both the problem and the solution, which they referred to as *social construction*. They suggested that these processes occur naturally and may or may not involve conscious reflection.

Building on work that describes how individuals get socialized into crafts (including midwives, tailors, and meat cutters) or communities (such as Alcoholics Anonymous) through a process of legitimate peripheral participation (Lave & Wenger, 1991), Etienne Wenger (1998) articulated a social theory of learning. For him, learning is an automatic feature of communities of practice. This explains, in part, why individuals rarely notice their own learning until they help someone else or stop to consider what they now know. Learning entails both involvement, with other community members, in the regular activities of a workplace community (participation) and the creation and use of abstractions—for example, tools, symbols, stories, and specialized language (reification). In addition, learning involves working with others in the community (mutual engagement); doing the work (joint enterprise); and becoming comfortable with using the tools and symbols of the work (shared repertoire).

These sociocultural theories of learning emphasize learning in the course of daily activity. They focus on how interactions with others, both those who are peers and those with more experience and technical knowledge, deepen individuals' knowledge, and facilitate collective problem solving. They also show how individuals actually create new knowledge and shape the work of a community of practice. These theories, however, do not fully conceptualize how *explicit* reflection or inquiry might contribute to learning from one's own practice.

Teacher Inquiry and Research

Within education, numerous academic researchers, sometimes building on the theorists in other fields, make a strong case for learning from practice (cf. Cochran-Smith & Lytle, 1993, 1999, 2009; Grimmett & MacKinnon, 1992; Zeichner, 1995). They add to our understanding of how teachers and other educators learn from practice, and how practitioners' knowledge and researchers' knowledge relate to each other. They pose important questions about knowledge in education: Who owns it? How do we get it? How can we collaborate on deepening knowledge?

Our research adds to the more general theories outlined above. First, and most simply, it illustrates how these ideas get enacted within education. Second, while acknowledging that professional learning can occur in practice, the research argues for the value of systematic and intentional inquiry into matters such as student learning, teaching, and leadership practice. Such practice-based, collaborative research potentially helps educators call into question their own frames and critique their own practice. Finally, this work illustrates how learning that takes place in local settings (such as among voluntary cross-school groups or within school teams) can become shareable and lead to improved teaching and schooling.

Although many have written about teacher research, we focus on Cochran-Smith and Lytle's ideas about teacher and practitioner research. Their commitment to educators' knowledge as a critical resource for the field, as evident in their own writing and their efforts to publish teachers' and other educators' research, aligns with the National Writing Project's central principles.

In their early work, Cochran-Smith and Lytle (1993) defined teacher research as "systematic, intentional inquiry by teachers about their own school and classroom work" (pp. 23–24). For them, inquiry involves educators constantly asking themselves critical questions about their work, rather than engaging in a time-bounded sequence of research steps (Cochran-Smith & Lytle, 1999, 2009). Just as Schön (1983) suggested that reflection-in-practice, specifically the framing and reframing of professional problems, is central to all professionals' work, Cochran-Smith and Lytle argued that learning from teaching forms teachers' primary task. They suggested that "building and sustaining intellectual communities of teacher researchers" is necessary to overcome the obstacles that teachers face in conducting research (pp. 85–86).

Cochran-Smith and Lytle emphasized the importance of teachers' own research as a critical source of public knowledge about the theories and practice of teaching. In a 1999 literature review, they described three contrasting conceptions of the relationship between knowledge and practice. A knowledge-*for*-practice view posits that knowledge for teaching comes from research and gets implemented by teachers; a knowledge-*in*-practice view emphasizes that teachers' expert craft knowledge, often developed over many years and articulated through reflection, represents a critical source of knowledge; and a knowledge-*of*-practice view, which they espoused, argues that teachers need to view their classrooms and schools as sites for learning, in order to generate knowledge and contribute to educational change.

In their most recent work, Cochran-Smith & Lytle (2009) expanded their conceptualization of the idea of inquiry as stance. Notably they shifted from the idea of "teacher research" to the more inclusive notion of "practitioner research." Building on their earlier work, Cochran-Smith and Lytle explained their assumptions:

> The key assumption is that a core part of the knowledge and expertise necessary for transforming practice and enhancing students' learning resides in the questions, theories, and strategies generated collectively by practitioners

themselves and in their joint interrogations of the knowledge, practices, and theories of others. (p. 124)

Cochran-Smith and Lytle's work emphasizes that educators not only learn from and critique their own practice as they engage in ongoing data collection, analysis, and reading of others' research and theory, but also create knowledge that is potentially useful beyond its local settings. This knowledge retains the concrete details and specific characteristics of its local origins, rather than being transformed into general principles.

LEARNING FROM PRACTICE: TEACHER-LEADERS' VOICES

Learning in the course of carrying out daily work represents a critical source of leadership learning for teacher-leaders. In this section we include four vignettes, preceded by brief contextual information, that highlight different dimensions of learning from practice.

Shayne Goodrum, a secondary district English coordinator, showed how she learned from teaching high school and reflecting on her work to build a team of district literacy specialists. In particular, she illustrated how Schön's process of reflection-in-action can unfold for teacher-leaders. Her urban school system serves more than 30,000 students, nearly 50% of whom are eligible for free and reduced-price lunch. The district is racially diverse: 54% African American, 23% Caucasian, 17% Hispanic/Latino, 3.5% Multiracial, and 2.5% Asian.

EVERYTHING I NEEDED TO KNOW WAS RIGHT THERE IN MY CLASSROOM

Shayne Goodrum

Every teacher lives for those moments when we know for sure something that happened in our class had an impact on someone's life, so one of my biggest fears about leaving the classroom to accept the job of district secondary English coordinator was that I'd no longer have that impact anywhere. I'd just be another of those bureaucrats sitting in the central office thinking up new ways to make teachers' lives more difficult. But I took the plunge, hoping that if I could remain connected to teachers, stay a teacher, perhaps I could show another way it could be done.

The new adolescent literacy initiative was put under my direction. At the time, our district had one person whose job was to provide support for teaching reading across content areas in all 10 of our middle schools. No one at the schools had any real expectations for the role. Under the new plan, several specialists would provide job-embedded professional development with follow-up coaching to our middle school teachers. With one person already in place, my assistant superintendent and I set out to hire new people to become a team under my leadership.

I surveyed my team. They were all solid educators with strong credentials and excellent recommendations. We could do this. But I underestimated the challenge of leading a team of professionals. Each specialist was assigned schools and schedules. We talked about our district philosophy, but the team still lacked a common focus and direction. Each one worked in the schools, but nothing really jelled. Some set up schedules of professional development for teachers, and others waited for something to be set up for them. One had difficulty building the relationships that open classroom doors to collaboration. We met each month and the meetings were cordial, but specialists often seemed to be trying to prove themselves, and I often heard one-upmanship when they told what they'd been doing. At the end of our meetings, I often felt empty. Something was missing in spite of my best efforts.

By the end of the year, it was clear there would be more changes. One specialist had decided to go to graduate school full time, and another accepted a job in another county. I couldn't help but wonder whether the lack of coherence contributed to the turnover. If I wanted things to turn out differently, to have a team that was focused and intentional in improving instruction for students, I had to act. I set aside my hesitancy to tell other professionals how to do their jobs and decided to take a more assertive role. I'd lead this team rather than just manage it.

I thought about my years in the classroom, considering what, as a teacher, I had been solely responsible for deciding and what I left open to student choice. This team was my new class, and I was responsible for establishing the structures that would ensure it achieved its goals. I needed to build a support structure so that each specialist felt safe making decisions but also knew the expectations for success. I pulled the two returning specialists into an advisory role, sharing my vision for a more cohesive team, one working in tandem to attain common goals. We talked about basic structures and my desire for an environment where we would collaborate and strive for excellence without being in competition.

After talking about what team members wished they had known when starting the job, we began planning an induction retreat for the team. The retreat would also begin shaping the team by helping us get to know one another and develop some team norms. Our team would meet twice a month, with one meeting designated for business, and the other devoted solely to professional growth for us as a team.

We decided our first professional development activity as a group would be reading and discussing Gloria Ladson-Billings's (1994) *Dreamkeepers: Successful Teachers of African American Children*, because not only was our district predominantly African American, but the book espouses some of the values I wanted for our team—equity and optimism with intellectually rigorous and challenging work. These values would be our bedrock, but without processes for putting them into practice, they'd just be so many platitudes; so each person would also participate in Facilitative Leadership training,* a leadership development program offered by the Interactive Institute for Social Change, during her first month on the job. This training would help team members learn skills to build and unite the diverse strengths and styles of the teachers in our schools.

My planning team decided that our meetings should, as much as possible, model what we wanted all teachers to do: use strategic teaching techniques to foster engaged literacy learning. We'd begin every meeting with a read-aloud and close with an evaluation using the Facilitative Leadership Plus/Delta tool to surface the strengths and challenges encountered in our work together. We made a rotating schedule so that each person would be responsible for some aspect of the meeting. One person would select and give the read-aloud, while another would have a time for leading us through an activity that worked well with teachers in the schools. In one presentation, we wrote on "handy tools," folded recycled copy paper that students lined up with the columns of print in their textbooks to jot questions, comments, and connections about the reading. These became so popular in one middle school that students asked to use them in all their classes.

For our professional development meetings, I took a more active role in determining the content based on my observations of the team, but each person shared in the presentation. I modeled in our first week's discussion of *Dreamkeepers*, but after that each person led the discussion, modeling the active learning strategies that we wanted to see in classrooms. I didn't want to neglect the relationship-building part of our meetings, but I knew that it was very easy for dynamic professionals to devolve into mostly social interaction, so I took on the role of guardian of our process, bringing us back when we strayed from our agenda. To build relationships, we began each meeting at noon with an optional brown-bag lunch. It was a happy medium, allowing us to share and bond, but preserving the integrity of our business.

The year went very well, as did the next. The team was strong, and our meetings gave each person individual time to shine with the group. Our structure not only melded us as a group, but gave cohesion to what we were trying to do in the schools. I watched each person grow. The rough edges between personalities softened, and we confronted issues before they reached crisis

---

*Facilitative Leadership is a trademarked program of Interaction Associates, 2007.

proportions. Over time, we began to see real impact in the schools. We saw students more actively engaged with learning and reading more text in class-rooms. Scores began to rise. Teachers counted on our team for new ideas and support. They helped mentor new teachers. Two of the team attended the Capital Area Writing Project one summer, opening them to the realization that they could coach teachers on writing instruction as well as reading.

I wish I could tell you that the team survived and was still impacting the district. But new leadership came in with different priorities and eliminated the coaching positions. Still, the power of what we built has endured. The team is scattered across several counties now, with a couple of us working at the state level, but we all remain in contact and gather occasionally to share a meal. While we all are in good work situations, every time we get together or see one another, someone comments on what a powerful experience it was and how we wish one day to have that dynamic again at work. Through it, I gained confidence in my capacity to lead adults.

Now I know that, just like in a classroom, achieving goals with adults requires intentionality and careful planning. While that planning often takes longer than one would imagine, its power extends well beyond the face-to-face time a group spends together; it forms the basis for the success of each person, as well as of the group. It's the leader's sometimes lonely job to create the blueprint, to decide where the solid walls stand, and what views the windows open. In my case, that meant creating a meeting structure that allowed each team member to share her knowledge. Only then could the group members contribute their individual designs to the work as a whole.

I've left the district now and work with teachers all across the state; but with every group, from 2 to 200, I'm always conscious that achieving goals and being effective never happens without consideration of individual needs. It's the leader's obligation to hold space for individual contributions while ensuring the momentum of the whole.

Even though I'm no longer working in a school with a bell that rings to begin class, I still have a classroom, just the walls and the ages of the students have changed. I'm still planning like a teacher, and I still have faith there's an impact on lives happening through my work.

Lucy Ware *contrasted her leadership work as a district literacy coach with her leadership as an elementary teacher. By reflecting on her leadership practice, she discovered how to build trust so that she and other teachers could learn from each other. Her vignette demonstrates how Brown and Duguid's (1996) concept "learning-in-working" may play out for teacher-leaders over time. Ware works in an urban district with approximately*

25,000 students, nearly 70% of whom qualify for free and reduced-price lunch. Her K–5 magnet elementary school's demographics mirror district averages; students outperform the district average on state reading and math tests.

LEARNING TO PROMOTE POSITIVE CHANGE AS A TEACHER

Lucy Ware

I am concerned and passionate about kids. As a student growing up on the same streets as my students today, I felt that school offered me nothing, so I am empathetic with today's urban youth. Many of the students we teach are knowledgeable in nontextbook ways, so as educators we need to tap into these strengths to help them learn. We need to help them see the relevance of what we teach, as well as the value that they contribute to their own education.

My Writing Project Summer Institute experience in 1987 shaped me as a teacher, giving the means to articulate my concerns and the resources to develop methods to define and make visible my goals. I learned the impact of structuring the learning environment to encourage inquiry, and the importance of building community. I believe that by improving education, children's lives can improve. Because of my beliefs, I'm interested in how teachers change their practice. How can I play a part in promoting positive change?

WORKING FROM THE OUTSIDE IN

I once thought that the most effective way to improve education was to reach as broad an audience as possible. For this reason I accepted a position as a demonstration teacher for the Division of Teaching, Learning and Assessment with my school district. I conducted on-site seminars, district workshops, and demonstration lessons; and developed instructional resources for teachers. I visited 10 to 12 schools a couple times each month, but soon I realized that I didn't know the staff or the students in the schools I serviced. I felt that I was just doing "drive-by" professional development because there wasn't any follow-up or support to sustain the work.

After 1 year, four elementary schools pooled their resources to purchase my time as a literacy coach. I had good rapport with the staff, and the principals valued my expertise because of my role as the codirector of the Western Pennsylvania Writing Project. I was considered a member of the school staff and given space in each building. I became familiar with the school's culture, staff, and students. I approached teachers with genuine interest in the areas they wanted support, and we planned together before I conducted demonstration lessons. I gave feedback on teachers' lessons as requested.

I learned early that coaching is primarily about building relationships. At one school teachers came together to eat lunch in small groups in their classrooms, while I ate alone in my office. This continued until I began pulling out nonreading-proficient second-grade students for reading interventions. Then I was invited to join their teachers' lunchtime group. It's about the work. If you're in the classroom working hard, you gain authenticity and respect. Coaches, because they work closely with teachers and principals and meet regularly with district curriculum developers, must be viewed as allies.

The following year, as a result of a districtwide school reform movement, my position changed and I was assigned the role of reading coach. Now as a reading coach I was no longer able to support writing instruction. Because the reading coach was only authorized to share specific practices, I often felt stifled. I knew the value of multiple approaches to reach the same goal, but I couldn't share this perspective with my fellow teachers. I felt more like a cop than a coach, so I resigned.

WORKING FROM THE INSIDE OUT

After resigning, I took a placement as a third-grade reading and language arts teacher at the Arts Academy (a pseudonym). I had learned so much and I was eager to put theory into practice. The academy has a large minority student population and a principal who believes in permitting teachers to teach to their passion. Four times weekly, I team-teach with two second-grade teachers. Once a week I teach writing in two first-grade classrooms, and frequently meet with these teachers during common planning time. At the academy I found a principal who respected the teaching of writing in a district that had eliminated writing from its 90-minute literacy block. Here I knew I could teach.

Now I work side-by-side with my peers. I make the work I do transparent during grade level and team meetings. Teachers observe, read student work on the walls, and ask for lesson plans, templates, or prompts that I use with my students. They come to me to ask for a book, discuss a genre, or ask how to help students revise their work; and this is my greatest compliment. I give it away, everything—my process, ideas, and suggestions—and it is reciprocated. I reveal my inadequacies and concerns, and they all know that I am with them. As classroom teachers, we can talk about the joys and the struggles in teaching in a way where judgment is reserved and it is safe to be real. We have a learning community and we each value it.

TEACHING TOGETHER

This is my 2nd year team-teaching writing with Ms. Debra Marsico (a pseudonym). Debra is the instructional teacher-leader and a veteran teacher. She is extremely organized and prides herself on having her lessons coordinated and prepared well in advance. One day when I walk into her second-grade classroom, she walks up and asks, "Do you mind helping me with the writing I'm doing? We're writing summer poems and I'm stuck. They keep writing stories." Although Debra is an excellent teacher, she usually follows my lead in writing instruction and seldom varies from our joint plans. I am pleased with her question and see it as a breakthrough.

I go to the board and remind the students how poems look differently on the page. I add that we focus on an image and that nouns and verbs help to build strong "word pictures." Then I describe how in poetry you may describe the nouns, and that it helps to include your senses. As examples, I read Langston Hughes's (1994) "April Rain Song" and a Christina Rossetti (2001) poem about the wind. I walk around and help individual students. Jorge (a pseudonym) isn't writing. I ask Jorge if the class can help him. He says yes. I go to the board and write the words Jorge has in his concept map, a prewriting strategy for organizing ideas, in a vertical pattern on the board. "Okay class, how can we give more information about the beach?" The students brainstorm to help Jorge elaborate his images, and many start over on their own pieces.

I tell the students to save their stories but have a try at the poetic form, eliminating unnecessary words and using their senses and imagination. Vi-Nuhan (a pseudonym) writes "the sun is my ceiling." Anna (a pseudonym) writes "the sun is like a kiss of lightning." Debra calls John (a pseudonym) to the author's chair. He reads his "story" and then he reads his poem. Debra highlights for the class the differences. As I leave Debra says, "Thank you. Now I know how to do it. I can use their prewriting to help them write poetry."

The following week, Debra suggests that we listen to the children read their adventure stories. I love it. This is the very thing I would ask another adult to do in my room—listen and respond.

As a classroom teacher, I am a model of what can be done. I have 28 students, but I also have writing workshops and read-arounds; and I publish an anthology of student work each year, all while having the same testing constraints and pressures as my peers. My students are my best ambassadors, writing at home, carrying their journals out to recess, and sharing writing they wrote with the principal and the entire school during assemblies. The fourth-grade reading teacher tells her student that she loves his "koi fish" journal entry, which the principal read during morning announcements. The fifth-grade language arts teacher remarks that one of my students' poems is unusual: "He has such a strong 'voice' for his age." The math teacher credits my students' success on the state math assessment with their ease with explaining their thinking in writing. The science teacher comments in the teachers' room that, "Ms. Ware's students are good writers and thinkers." Leah (a pseudonym), a first grader, says, "Ms. Ware, I'm going to be a writer when I grow up. I'm going to put your name in the beginning to say that Ms. Ware taught me how to write." I am continually learning and finding joy in the process.

My teacher friends share their ideas with me because they know that my enthusiasm will match theirs. Hopefulness is a rare commodity in today's classrooms. I've learned that it's the conversations and the shared work that help teachers grow in their practice. As an outsider you can inform, cajole, or even threaten. But change in practice happens only when teachers decide to change. The academy is a place where change happens as teachers refine their practice together. I feel I am a collaborative coach who cares deeply about children and the teachers who guide their development. I've narrowed my lens from a broad landscape view to one that allows me to see individual faces; my work is more effective now. As a teacher and colleague, I play a part in promoting positive change.

Anne H. Aliverti, *a district new-teacher mentor, developed her ability to tailor her support to meet the strengths and needs of 1st-year teachers by asking questions, observing closely, and drawing on her network of resources. Specifically, she showed how she learned to ask questions of Ishmel (a pseudonym), an eighth-grade teacher at an urban middle school that serves students who are racially diverse and 70% of whom are eligible for free or reduced-price lunch.*

NOW YOU SEE ME, NOW YOU DON'T

Anne H. Aliverti

As a mentor, I have the privilege to support 1st-year teachers, who have traded in long hours in the library for Sallie Mae loans and teaching certificates. My district's mentor program offers instructional support, coaching, and collaboration, whichever services teachers need to sustain themselves through the Dante's Inferno that is the 1st year of teaching. Although I was hired for my expertise in middle school language arts, my 1st-year caseload included teachers well outside of my comfort zone.

CHECK YOUR NOTES, HOMIE

At the new-teacher orientation, I encountered a reporter from the local newspaper bobbing among the 100-plus teachers, looking for someone to interview about the trials of starting a teaching career. Although I had just met him, I introduced the reporter to Ishmel (a pseudonym), a newly hired eighth-grade teacher with a quiet, friendly demeanor. A week later, dressed in black slacks, a teal dress shirt, and a tie, Ishmel appeared self-assuredly on the front page under the headline "Natural Born Teacher." My excitement with Ishmel's debut was quickly followed by panic. What would I have to offer a *natural born teacher*?

During my first observation, this natural born teacher rapped a history lesson to his class. As I watched his students, some flushed and appeared embarrassed for him at first. Then two boys exchanged glances, one saying to the other, "He's sick." Countering the typical needs of 1st-year teachers, Ishmel and I would not be working on his class management. When I met with Ishmel, we started by identifying what he thought was going well. Together, we cited many aspects of quality teaching: cooperative learning, active engagement, and student-centered, constructivist approaches. In recognizing the challenges, however, Ishmel remained quiet for a moment. I offered some ideas: perhaps planning or assessing? Silence.

Effective mentors absorb a teacher's scene and, when necessary, stand back to give time and space for new teachers to take risks and to learn from both their successes and their failures. Ishmel's school boasted a streamlined teaching staff, which met regularly and agreed on systemic pedagogical approaches and units of study. Ishmel seemed impervious to the shrapnel of the early days in the profession. I felt superfluous in his world. Yet I continually reminded myself that our relationship was not predicated on my needs, so I persisted.

As our time together unfolded, Ishmel grew accustomed to seeing me, and I improved my skills to ask specific questions based on my observations. Over time, I asked questions such as:

- How do you think the lesson went?
- In what ways did students meet your expectations and learning goals? How do you know?
- How do you attend to students who appear confused or disengaged?
- How might you follow this lesson?
- What conclusions might you draw from my observational data?
- How does what happened today relate to your professional goals?

I sensed these questions enabled him to articulate his concerns and approach them from the perspective of problem solving. Acting more as a consultant, I suggested materials and resources. Toward the end of the school year, Ishmel and I spent a day touring different schools to watch exemplary teachers. Removing ourselves from his classroom setting and having more time, I discovered that this man of steel had his own ordeals. Two car accidents in the winter, along with the pressures of teaching, had almost taken him "over the edge." He thought he had revealed this earlier, but I only recall hearing, "Everything's fine." It occurred to me that, given Ishmel's *readiness to learn*, had I planned our visitations earlier in the year, I might have helped to advance his practice further. He might have even confided more in me.

Teachers ascend to mentoring positions because they have demonstrated high-quality instruction, innovative problem solving, and a propensity for helping colleagues—leadership. Ironically, effective mentoring hinges on the ability to remove oneself from that identity in order that new teachers discover their own practical solutions to their craft. In reflecting on these mentoring relationships, I have come to recognize why I constantly seek opportunities to lead. A Pablo Picasso quotation sums it up best: "I am always doing that which I cannot do, in order that I may learn how to do it" (Picasso, n.d.).

Scott Peterson, *an upper-elementary district curriculum director, demonstrated how his curricular experimentation with an experienced colleague generated knowledge that would be useful for other teachers in the district. In his vignette, Peterson created a composite portrait of his 10 years as a district curriculum coordinator. Peterson worked in a rapidly growing district that serves just under 4,000 students, 90% of whom are Caucasian. The district, which draws students from both suburban and rural areas, has a reputation for strong educational programs.*

Keeping One Foot Inside the Door: What I Learned About Teacher Leadership

Scott Peterson

Stepping out of the classroom into any kind of leadership position was never part of my long-range plans. I enjoyed the challenges and satisfactions of working in the classroom too much. I had served on a wide variety of committees and enjoyed having an impact beyond my classroom on schoolwide practices. The curriculum positions in our districts, though, were the classic hodgepodge mix of clerical and administrative tasks, such as writing curriculum maps and guides, purchasing supplies, administering our statewide assessments, selecting text books, placing students, dealing with dissatisfied parents, and anything else that could be thrown into the pot. It was a lightning rod of a position, attracting all tasks and responsibilities too charged to handle elsewhere.

I wasn't completely surprised, though, when my principal strolled into my room on a muggy August afternoon several years ago and asked me point blank if I would consider being the curriculum director for the upper elementary grades in our district. Our previous director, the third in 9 years, had recently flown off to greener pastures. Given my expertise in literacy techniques, interest in curriculum issues, and inside knowledge of the needs of our district, he thought I would be an excellent choice. I told him I was deeply flattered by the offer, but I had been teaching so long that I had chalk dust in my veins, and the position was just too far removed from classroom teaching to be to my liking.

I did say that I might be interested in a different kind of leadership position. I explained that the position he was offering did a fine job of answering two key curriculum questions: What do we teach and when do we teach it? The problem, though, was that the position did not go far enough. Once the curriculum had been written and put in handsome binders with multicolored tabs, pacing charts created to move things along in a timely manner, and commercial texts and supplies purchased, the committee would close shop and return to the classroom, the process grinding to a halt. What was needed, I felt, was a position that went beyond the what and where of curriculum and dealt directly with the question of how to teach. Somewhere along the line, someone had to translate all the paperwork into research-based strategies and activities that would provide the best learning possible. We needed a bridge between the curriculum guide and what goes on in the classroom. Until we had a leadership position with one foot firmly planted inside the classroom, all the paperwork would be little more than smoke and mirrors. My principal said, "Let me talk to a few people about this."

One month later I began my new position in curriculum and staff development.

COLLABORATING WITH TEACHERS

Today I am working in a second-grade classroom, trying to develop a writing project that will get these students where they need to go. It is not easy by any means. Getting thoughts down on paper in good order and with style is difficult at any age, much less for a class of squirmy 8-year-olds. The task we are working on is further complicated by the fact that it is dictated to us by the high-stakes testing in our state, and is complex, daunting, and as developmentally inappropriate as can be. Once again, we are starting at a place that no reasonable educator would ever consider; but, as all good teachers know, sometimes circumstances beyond our control dictate our beginning point.

The activity the classroom teacher and I have created for this class of second graders is a little too complex and demanding at this stage of development. Several of them take to it pretty well. They soar and dance above the crowd and can't wait to sit in the author's chair and sing their glorious songs. For the bulk of the students, a dim light is beginning to glow, and they will eventually do nicely, provided we give them enough guidance and support. Those on the outer fringes are barely hanging on by their fingernails and will succeed only if we revamp the activity to meet their needs—and maybe not then.

After school tonight, the teacher and I will adjust and simplify this activity so it will rope in a larger share of her students. She is a veteran writing-process teacher and a joy to collaborate with. She thinks of writing not as a skill that must be mastered for high-stakes testing but as a tool to celebrate and enhance life. Her mind is like a sponge, ready and willing to absorb anything that improves the quality of writing, and her positive attitude shines through the eyes of her students whenever I have the pleasure of working in her classroom. My expertise lies in the upper grades, and working with second graders is as new to me as working with aliens from outer space. Their endless flow of kinetic energy makes it like working in a room full of bouncing ping-pong balls. I will tap into her thick notebook of knowledge and experience to fine-tune this activity so it will work as smoothly as possible in her classroom. I know this will happen because we have worked together before and are used to the collaboration process—progress slowly emerging out of chaos and confusion.

When the dust begins to settle and that gut-level feeling of success emerges from our efforts, second-grade teachers from the district will come and observe the activity in action in another classroom. Afterward, we will sit around long conference tables with our lunches spread out in front of us to process and reflect on what they observed. We will do what good teachers have done since the beginning of time—sit down eye-to-eye and knee-to-knee, and pool our collective knowledge to sculpt this project into the exact shape we want it to be. We will add a minilesson on strong leads so these second graders can launch their stories in the best possible way. We will once again model the use of thought—shots and snapshots to add depth, details, and voice to their writing. We will tighten up the scaffolding so that the organization and structure of their pieces clarifies and supports their narratives. When the hand holding the pencil creating this activity shifts from mine to all of ours, when we all feel a common ownership of this strategy and are vested in its success, we will go back and apply it in the classroom. A seed has been planted. Seed by seed we will repeat this process, cultivating and nourishing each one until we have the curriculum we want.

MY LEADERSHIP PROCESS

This is the way the leadership process works for me. It starts with a long, hard look at the issues that are rippling down toward our classroom. Next,

I provide inservice professional development for our staff about the things coming our way. Finally, we will sit down to meld this information together to create the research-based strategies that will enhance the learning in our classrooms and get our students where we want them to go in the best possible way. When all is said and done, I will take the show on the road and model these activities in the classrooms around the district to spread the seed as far and wide as I can.

This process isn't easy. Slow and cumbersome at times, difficult to see the light at the end of the tunnel other times. The frustrations of dealing with so many different people and the demands heaped on our classroom by forces higher up the educational food chain are enough to keep me up at night.

I have to admit, though, that the job has its moments. When I see the shine in Helen's (a pseudonym) eyes as she shares her detailed and richly developed description of the playground, when I watch Aria (a pseudonym) sit in the author's chair quivering with excitement because she can't wait to share her ideas with the rest of the world, when Frank (a pseudonym) stands up and shares a lead to his personal narrative about the field trip to the butterfly house that is so clear and sharp that it far surpasses the one developed by his instructor (me), and when I see all this take root and spread from classroom to classroom, it's sometimes hard to believe they pay me for this job, so deeply satisfying and fulfilling it is. This is the way it should have been when I began my career almost 30 years ago, and this is the way it will be in the future if I have anything to say about it.

LEARNING TO USE LAYERED KNOWLEDGE IN UNCERTAIN AND UNIQUE SITUATIONS: OUR ANALYSIS

Teacher-leaders draw on a wide range of knowledge and experience in their day-to-day work. The vignette writers showed their knowledge of pedagogy and content (Nelson & Sassi, 2005; Shulman, 1986; Stein & Nelson, 2003), about adult learning theory (Bransford, Brown, & Cocking, 1999), and about how collaboration and community develop. They learned from past and current practice. Many engaged in explicit research and reflection about what works as well as about what they needed to improve to more effectively serve their peers and students. And they attended to the particular questions and concerns in their local situations.

Collectively the research literature outlined above frames five ideas related to how professionals—especially educators—learn from practice:

1. learning from working,
2. learning with and from others day to day,

3. learning through addressing unique local problems of practice,
4. bringing their own and others' past experiences to bear on leadership challenges, and
5. learning through reflection and inquiry.

We see these processes at work in the stories told by the teacher-leaders with whom we worked. Their leadership learning is rooted in their day-to-day practice and becomes visible to them and to us through their writing and reflection. Our analysis incorporates examples from the vignettes in this chapter as well as from other vignettes.

Framing Leading as a Problem of Teaching

Just as the vignette writers maintained their identities as teachers even as they accepted a range of leadership roles, they often viewed their leadership challenges as teaching challenges. Their processes of framing and addressing problems paralleled the steps Schön (1983) observed practitioners from other fields taking to solve complex local problems.

For example, Shayne Goodrum, a district curriculum coordinator, realized after a disappointing year that the facilitation challenges she faced with her team of adolescent literacy specialists were similar to those she encountered in her classroom. She illustrated how professionals can reflect on and reframe the challenges that they face in order to find solutions. Initially, Goodrum believed that her role involved hiring good professionals, setting aside time to meet, and stepping aside so they could do their work. She framed the situation as one of letting professionals be professional.

But although the literacy team met regularly and the specialists treated each other cordially, the meetings didn't help them work more effectively with teachers in their classrooms. Upon reflection, Goodrum came to see the problem and her role as a leader differently. She identified the ways in which her team leadership was similar to her work as a high school teacher; in Schön's parlance, she reframed the problem so that it could be solved. She then set about using some of the strategies she had used to build community in her high school classroom with her team: establishing the tone and structure of the team; giving the team an opportunity to create its own norms; and selecting a common text.

Here Goodrum, like Schön, conducted a series of experiments, evaluated their effects on the team's work, and found that she was pleased with the results. In summary, Goodrum's solution centered on creating a formal structure to support literacy specialists to engage in collaborative storytelling so that they could learn with and from each other, an example of sociocultural learning.

Learning to Lead by Leading

> I learned to lead by leading, and have been empowered to use my talents.
> (Smith, 2006)

The vignettes illustrate different dimensions of learning from working, including learning by gradually taking on greater responsibility in a given setting, learning from realizing what makes some approaches ineffective, and learning through trial and error. C. Lynn Jacobs, a high school English Language Development teacher, described becoming a leader in her Writing Project site. Another teacher-leader recognized Jacobs' potential contributions and invited her to coplan and colead a professional development institute. At the time, Jacobs had limited professional development experience. Initially, she felt awkward and believed she had little to contribute. Her colleague gave her "a little something to present" and Jacobs began speaking up about how ideas related to English learners. Through these small steps, Jacobs learned how to design and facilitate professional development. Over time she mentored others into Writing Project leadership positions. Jacobs reflected,

> I realize that [my colleague's] mentorship had everything to do with my growth as a leader in the Writing Project. She saw something in me that I didn't see, and just kept pushing at me until I could let it out and stand with it. She made room for me to assume a role of leadership in the Writing Project site at the time I was ready to do so.

Jacobs showed how she slowly took on more responsibility while observing and learning from those who had more experience designing and facilitating professional development; sociocultural theorists call this process *legitimate peripheral participation* (Lave & Wenger, 1991). Jacobs illustrated how she gradually learned Writing Project approaches to leading and designing professional development (see Chapter 2 for additional information about Writing Project practices), with the support of a key mentor.

Lucy Ware, a veteran urban elementary school teacher and former district literacy coach, learned how to effectively provide instructional leadership among her peers through a process of trial and error. While working as a district literacy coach, Ware found out that building relationships and demonstrating credibility as a teacher were critical to being able to successfully share ideas with teachers. She built effectively on this insight when she returned to classroom teaching and found ways to share her expertise in teaching writing with her colleagues.

Specifically, Ware pointed to the importance of collaborative reflection and inquiry in developing as a teacher and a leader. Ware's collaboration with her accomplished veteran colleague, Ms. Marsico, involved the same kind of collaborative problem solving that Brown and Duguid's (1996) copier repair technicians engaged in. Ms. Marsico confided that she was "stuck" and could not figure out how to help her second graders shift from writing stories to crafting poems. Honoring Marsico's request for help, Ware asked students to share their stories, and then helped the students turn their stories into poetry. Here, Ware's modeling helped Marsico teach poetry on her own and find her own solutions to her teaching challenge. In this example, Marsico expanded her teaching repertoire and Ware strengthened her ability to facilitate her colleagues' learning by "learning-in-working" (Brown & Duguid, 1996, p. 59). Further, Ware's work exemplifies a "knowledge-of-practice" perspective on teacher learning (Cochran-Smith & Lytle, 1999). She demonstrated that she and her colleagues had the capacity for "transforming practice and enhancing students' learning" (Cochran-Smith & Lytle, 2009, p. 124).

Engaging in Reflection and Inquiry

Theories about learning from practice highlight both reflection that takes place in the moment, and more sustained, systematic approaches to inquiry and reflection that support professionals in learning. Throughout the vignettes we see writers reflecting on and sometimes purposefully researching their leadership work. Lynne Dorfman, a school-based writing support teacher, described how she worked for 2 years to establish a writers workshop and the use of writers' notebooks in every classroom. Dorfman drew on many past experiences in her own classroom and with the Writing Project. What is notable about Dorfman's vignette, however, is her reflective stance. At each point, she showed her keen awareness of what teachers responded to, what they were trying in their classrooms, and what they left by the wayside. Dorfman portrayed a morning professional development meeting when her colleague shared writing from his own and his students' writing notebooks; all of a sudden teachers "who were not as comfortable with writing were now scribbling furiously in their notebooks." Dorfman translated this observation into a guiding principle: "[W]hen someone else demonstrated, talked about his writing, talked about the students' writing, interest stirred. I needed to think about these meetings as a collaborative leadership—bringing in more writers to model the power of writing."

Dorfman was tenacious in working toward her goal; while she recognized that teachers were trying some ideas, she was unwilling to give up until everyone used writers notebooks daily. She kept looking for approaches and eventually succeeded. This example shows how taking an inquiry stance—questioning what is and isn't working, observing closely, and trying out new things—can support teacher-leaders in learning from practice.

Similarly, Anne Aliverti described how reflecting on her mentorship of new teachers helped her become more effective. Initially, she expressed uncertainty about how to support a new teacher, Ishmel, who exhibited strong teaching practices from the outset and who did not articulate his questions. By reflecting on her relationship with Ishmel, Aliverti realized that she could elicit his concerns by asking questions that prompted him to reflect on his teaching. In this example, as in that of Ware's collaboration with her veteran colleague, both Aliverti and her new colleague improved their practice by engaging in reflection.

Weaving Together Multiple Sources of Knowledge

Schön (1983), along with Cochran-Smith and Lytle (2009), argued that practitioners create knowledge that is potentially useful beyond their own settings. Across the vignettes, the teacher-leaders wrote about drawing on teachers' knowledge—both their own and others'—to improve practice. In addition, almost all the authors also reported integrating ideas from research, policy, and theory. The vignette authors did not implement practices and ideas developed by researchers in a step-by-step way; rather they constantly tested and retested ideas to see how they fit with the particular children and adults with whom they worked and in the settings in which they worked. As they led, they figured out how to use many forms of knowledge in ways that were flexible and adaptable. This approach to using and developing knowledge is central to the National Writing Project's approach to teaching (Stokes, 2005).

In supporting the development of Masters in Arts in Teaching (MAT) candidates, Linda Tatman (Chapter 1) spent time learning about their teaching questions and successes. As she built rapport with them, she shared ideas from her own teaching (e.g., including lesson plans related to their interests) and from research (e.g., Harvey Daniels' work about literature circles). Rather than telling them what to do, however, Tatman found ways to share ideas that allowed teachers to make them their own. Tatman reflected on what she and her MAT students learned from her approach:

> I began to realize . . . I did have new and useful ideas to contribute. . . . Because I asked questions about incorporating new strategies and texts rather than merely telling them what to do, they were better able to think, evaluate, and reflect. They felt they had permission to take what I had to offer and rework it to meet their needs.

Here, Tatman learned both what the teachers needed and what she had to offer; she shared a broad range of knowledge to help them address their own teaching questions.

Scott Peterson, a district curriculum coordinator, also drew on a wide range of knowledge sources to address an omnipresent teaching challenge: how to approach mandates and turn written curriculum into teaching practices that support authentic student learning. This vignette shows how teacher-leaders learn from a variety of sources. Peterson worked collaboratively with teachers to carry out teaching experiments. He described working with a second-grade teacher to design a writing lesson that would address his state's standards. They considered research on best practice and the state's mandates, and then cotaught the class. They realized that the task they had created was "a little too complex and demanding at this stage of [the students'] development." After school, they sat down "to adjust and simplify this activity so it [would] rope in a larger share of . . . students." Once they polished the work, they shared it with other second-grade teachers, who in turn critiqued the work and had an opportunity to adjust the lesson to meet the needs of their own students. In sum, Peterson illustrated how educators draw on a range of ideas as they engage in collaborative learning.

Both Peterson and Tatman incorporated research, policy, their own and other teachers' practice, and inquiry into their approach to facilitating teachers' learning and their development of their own practice. Peterson's and Tatman's approaches to knowledge use and development, along with those of other vignette writers, are consistent with the idea that "knowledge is always forming and can never be truly whole or complete, both because teaching is a continually challenging and surprising enterprise and because knowledge itself continually evolves" (Stokes, 2005, p. 35). Likewise, leadership knowledge, which is intimately connected with knowledge of teaching and learning, can never be complete.

SUMMARY

The literature and vignettes highlight two important processes involved in learning from practice. First, learning from practice gets embedded in daily work and is a fundamental process that cuts across different types of work environments. The vignette authors gradually built a repertoire of practice as they sought to reframe and solve problems, and as they collaborated with others. Second, learning from practice can involve deliberate and systematic inquiry for the purpose of creating social change "to improve the day-to-day school lives and futures of the students and families with whom they work" (Cochran-Smith & Lytle, 2009, p. 150). Through reflecting on their own work and engaging their colleagues in reflective practice, the vignette authors aimed to help students grow as readers, writers, and thinkers.

Epilogue

Three overarching ideas emanate from our study of teacher-leaders and the writing of this book: a reframing of teacher leadership, network participation as a foundation for leadership, and the importance of learning from both academic research and teachers' knowledge.

REFRAMING TEACHER LEADERSHIP

An important part of our collaboration with the teacher-leaders in our project centered on reframing a definition of leadership that reflected their core principles about students, teaching, learning, and professional development, as well as their approaches to working with others. Through the vignettes and a series of focus group conversations, together, we defined teacher leadership in a way that emphasizes a focus on students, collaboration with teachers, and a commitment to ongoing learning.

Some authors assumed, in the beginning, that leadership meant holding positional authority, working hierarchically, having all the answers, and being solely in charge. As we worked together, we learned that teacher leadership reflects several core principles that are exemplified in their work:

- Advocating what's right for students;
- Opening the classroom door and going public with teaching;
- Working "alongside" teachers and leading collaboratively;
- Taking a stand; and
- Learning and reflecting on practice as a teacher and leader.

During the focus group interviews that we conducted with 28 of the vignette authors at the final writing retreat, these teacher-leaders articulated what it means to be a leader and how they see themselves as leaders. For some, these were new insights, informed through writing and conversation about the vignettes; for others, this thinking extended their previous reflection on their work as leaders.

Advocating What's Right for Students

Teacher-leaders put forward a vision for education grounded in what is best for students. Their vision grows out of their day-to-day experiences in their own classrooms as well as their understanding of research and other professional reading about excellent teaching practice. These teacher-leaders read broadly about a wide range of topics, including but not limited to, teaching writing and literacy, integrating writing in the content areas, learning theory, school change, and the like. One veteran high school teacher reflected,

> But for me, going back to the classroom is the thing. That's the real thing. . . . I want to give them [my students] everything I have . . . and to open the door for them. . . . That's the pivot for me. And that's what gives power to the teacher-leader. (Teacher, June 2006)

We see this commitment to high-quality teaching and learning woven throughout the vignettes collected here. Austen Reilley (Chapter 1) showed how her girls' afterschool writing club built middle school girls' passion for writing and developed their self-confidence. Her positive experiences with the club led to schoolwide changes that improved opportunities to learn to write for all children in the school. Deidré Farmbry (Chapter 3) illustrated how she carried her commitments as a teacher into positions with formal authority—as a principal and district administrator. She worked hard to keep from "getting lost" while attending to issues of safety, racism, and governance and to keep her focus on improving teaching and learning for students.

Opening the Classroom Door, Going Public With Teaching

Sharing one's teaching, and the successes of one's students, serves as a powerful mode of teacher leadership. One vignette author explained her motivation:

> You believe in something and you want to spread it, so even if you just spread it to one person, you feel like you're making a difference. Whereas there are teachers in my school who I think are great teachers, but all they do is go and close their door. (Teacher, June 2006)

Christy James (Chapter 3) used her position as a master teacher to make visible the ways in which she integrates reading and writing into her day-to-day social studies curriculum. She opened her classroom door gently—first helping her colleagues see why her approach mattered, then modeling one strategy at a time during meetings, and finally making an open invitation to stop by her classroom. Following her example, her colleagues opened up their own teaching, sharing their efforts to integrate reading and writing during monthly department meetings. Similarly, Lucy Ware (Chapter 4) took advantage of opportunities to coteach with colleagues and collaborate with them to support elementary students' development as writers. She not only gave away her own ideas, she championed the work of her colleagues. Going public with teaching means both sharing one's own practice *and* inviting colleagues to share.

Working Alongside Teachers, Leading Collaboratively

The teacher-leaders used a variety of phrases to characterize the collaborative, behind-the-scenes nature of their work: "working alongside," "grassroots," "collaborative," "teacher-to-teacher," "quiet," "behind the scenes," and "helping people find their strengths." For them, leadership takes the form of doing what needs to be done and working hard both in and out of their classrooms. Teacher leadership is egalitarian and respectful of teachers' knowledge. Many times it goes unacknowledged:

> It helps you to see the value in supporting your colleagues, so that you don't have to get the credit. Because if you help someone else and they do a wonderful job and they get accolades, it makes you feel good because you helped support them. (Teacher, June 2006)

Those who moved into positions of formal leadership wrestled with how to maintain their commitment to collaboration with teachers while fulfilling expectations for formal leadership. Ronni Tobman Michelen (Chapter 2) characterized this as an internal conversation among three voices—teacher, writing project teacher-consultant, and vice principal. She showed how she carefully thought through inviting teachers to colead professional development sessions.

Taking a Stand

While the vignette authors highlighted the behind-the-scenes nature of their leadership, they also acknowledged the importance of staying true to their principles and standing up for what they believe. One person defined a teacher-leader as a "person who doesn't avoid struggle, somebody who just takes risks, someone who tries to expand justice, guide others" (retired teacher, focus group interview, June 2006). Christy James (Chapter 3) portrayed how she worked to keep a focus on integrating reading and writing in the social studies curriculum even after the district decided that all middle schools should implement a test preparation program for the 5 months leading up to the state social studies test. While James could have complied with the new mandates or hidden her department's true work, she instead chose to be direct with the district administrator. She described what they were doing, explained why they were sticking with an integrated approach, and invited the administrator to see the work in action. Her approach created space to do what was best for teachers and students.

Learning and Reflecting on Practice as a Teacher and a Leader

Finally, teacher-leaders constantly seek to broaden their knowledge base. They read widely and stay informed of new research and professional literature related to their field. They reflect on their teaching and on the work that they do with their peers. They constantly seek to improve their teaching and leadership practice. They emphasize that they do not have all the answers and often turn to others. In the focus groups, several people connected this learning stance to their involvement in the Writing Project:

> I think another very important facet of the Writing Project is that it is research-based and we read together. Because we have that understanding of the importance of the research, we individually and collectively seek out new ways of doing things and staying informed, staying on the cutting edge, not accepting the status quo, "just because we've done it this way for so long" attitude. (School-based literacy coach, June 2006)

Learning and reflection thread through the vignettes. Mimi Dyer (Chapter 3) learned how to be a more collaborative and effective literacy leader through failing as a department chair and then taking a step back to rethink her approach. Deidré Farmbry (Chapter 3), Christy James (Chapter 3), and Austen Reilley (Chapter 1) demonstrated how they turned to professional literature and used it to build their own knowledge base as well as build the capacity of others. Yarda Leflet (Chapter 1), Paul Epstein, Kim Larson, and Ronni Tobman Michelen (all Chapter 3) illustrated how they sought to develop the leadership capacities of others and in the process grew as leaders themselves.

These vignettes illustrate in teacher-leaders' own voices what teacher leadership is and how it grows. For these authors, teacher leadership connects to teachers' core commitments, respects collaborative and quiet approaches to working with others, and emphasizes the necessity of continuing to learn. These core principles are manifest in the way these teacher-leaders write about and see their work. They are adamant about standing up for students and taking a stand when they think that the pedagogy and the practices they use are more effective than those proposed by policy makers. And they are constant in their position that collaborative work and working side by side with peers is a powerful way to lead. And finally, they feel responsible for facilitating opportunities for teachers to open up their classroom work and examine it publicly. This collaborative and advocacy stance characterizes their definition of teachers who lead.

NETWORK PARTICIPATION: A FOUNDATION FOR LEADERSHIP

While the vignettes focus on a slice of each author's life as a teacher-leader, many writers described explicitly how participation in the National Writing Project served as a foundation for their work. Of the 31 vignette authors, 23 wrote explicitly about how the Writing Project influences their work as leaders. In addition, the vignette authors rated their Writing Project experience as influencing and informing their work in 98% of the positions they held during their careers following their participation in the Invitational Institute.

They talked about how they learned to build collaborative work, explaining that they expected to have conflict but knew they had many colleagues whom they could call upon to help them work through their problems. Many referred to the fact that NWP members read research and other literature so that they can keep on broadening their perspective. Others showed how the group processes that they had learned in the Writing Project—writing together, sharing what they had written with others, feeling comradeship in going public with their stories, teaching each other—became part of how they worked with others. Still others described collaborating with Writing Project colleagues to figure out how to address conflicting demands and to continue to grow as teachers and as leaders.

Although our project is set in the Writing Project, it may indeed be the case that other networks give people opportunities to learn apart from their daily context and to experience more collaborative and supportive ways of working. Because such opportunities support rather than thwart social learning, the practices encountered seem to become a part of the repertoire of teachers who lead. Belonging to a network that focuses on strong teacher participation with norms of inquiry helps socialize teachers into thinking (and acting) in ways better aligned with the larger goals of continuous improvement of practice, and provides opportunity for practice in how to organize these experiences for others. In many ways, these teacher-leaders, both through their actions and through their writing, help build teacher knowledge of how to lead.

LEARNING FROM BOTH ACADEMIC RESEARCH
AND TEACHERS' KNOWLEDGE

As we read academic research and the teacher-leaders' vignettes alongside each other, we noticed how each called our attention to different things. Academic research knowledge typically prizes the general and conceptual, while teacher knowledge emphasizes the experiential, complex, and contextualized dailiness of the work. Academic research helps us understand how central leadership challenges have been studied across time and in different settings, and thus helped us pose new questions about the vignettes and situate what we were learning in a larger history. The vignettes (and teacher knowledge more generally) give us a picture of the social, intellectual, and emotional story of how human beings nuance and challenge these frames. Both help us understand how teachers learn to lead; both help educators take hold of ideas and contribute to developing the knowledge base.

Identity

Academic research teaches us that identity is not fixed; it is inherently social; and there is room for change. It shows that adopting an identity shapes individuals' sense of agency. The vignettes make visible how these ideas work for teacher-leaders. We see Elizabeth Davis (Chapter 1) create the conditions for her students to develop a sense of agency. Further, the vignettes illustrate the struggles in this process. Austen Reilley (Chapter 1) wonders whether she should be a teacher, but as girls become more confident and boys more proficient writers her belief was strengthened that she could make a difference. Similarly, Linda Tatman (Chapter 1) questioned whether she would be able to build community with the teachers who were her Master of Arts in Teaching students in the same way she had accomplished this with her high school students.

The vignettes also show us how teachers often hold on to and draw on their identities as teachers as they move into leadership roles. Yarda Leflet (Chapter 1) engaged in both internal and external struggle and questioning as she moved from high school teacher to assistant principal: Why is the behavior of my peers so different now that I am an assistant principal? How can I use what I know from teaching and the Writing Project in my new position?

Collegiality and Community

The research on how to build collegiality and community describes how colleagueship is made up of such things as building a shared language, planning and designing materials together, and teaching and observing one another.

The vignettes reveal what colleagueship looks like, how it is organized, and what strategies are used; they also show how teachers develop their skills to build community.

Paul Epstein (Chapter 2) highlighted how he started by informally collaborating with his peers, encouraging them to try new practices for teaching writing and to consider leading peers. He showed how he and his colleague drew on Writing Project practices to develop a sense of community in a study group that teachers had previously seen as complying with a mandate.

Kim Larson (Chapter 2) showed how developing community among teachers could translate to other professional settings. Academic research aptly describes what teachers do when they become colleagues, and teacher knowledge rounds out the practical means for building colleagueship in particular contexts. The vignettes also teach us new lessons about developing the skills, knowledge, and experience to build community.

Conflict

Conflict theorists teach us how they conceptualize conflict, exploring how stereotypes and power contribute to it. They also highlight that knowledge, skills, and strategies can be developed to help people learn from and productively resolve conflict. Teacher-leaders who experienced conflict described particular situations in their context where conflicts arose and the different ways they handled it. Mimi Dyer (Chapter 3) failed to resolve her philosophical conflicts with her department, but through reflection became more skillful at building community and resolving similar conflicts. Deidré Farmbry (Chapter 3) figured out how to clear away the myths that were seen as absolutes in a school district that had denied African American students a proper and equitable education.

Again we see the general, theoretical, and conceptual nature of academic research teaching us about conflict and the variety of approaches people have taken to understanding how to resolve it. We learn from teacher knowledge how teacher-leaders think about conflict, and the nuances of how teacher-leaders learn to negotiate, handle, and resolve particular clashes over roles, relationships, prejudice, pedagogy, and power in their particular contexts.

Practice

In the past several decades, researchers have sought to understand how people learn through analyzing their own practice. Ideas like the "reflective practitioner" and "taking an inquiry stance" have in many respects become accepted knowledge in education. Social theories of learning have begun to infuse the literature, teaching us how people in organizations where jobs are nonroutine, changeable, and complex learn from one another in communities of practice.

The vignettes reveal how teacher-leaders learn how to become more effective through their practice. Lucy Ware (Chapter 4) realized that she could support deeper change by leaving her district coaching position and returning to the classroom. Anne Aliverti (Chapter 4) learned how to shape her support for each new teacher she mentored to specifically meet their questions and needs; in doing so, she both drew on her own classroom experience and sought to draw on a wider range of resources including other teachers and professional reading.

The role of reflection also becomes evident, as Shayne Goodrum (Chapter 4) learned from literacy team meetings that prioritized socializing rather than professional learning and figured out how to create a more effective learning community for the middle school literacy coaches in her district.

Finally, the vignettes illustrate how teacher-leaders seek to formally draw on and share teacher knowledge to improve teaching and learning. Scott Peterson (Chapter 4) described his collaboration with another veteran teacher to create practices that bridge the written standards and curriculum with the real world of the classroom. Academic research and the vignettes together help reveal the subtle, often tacit dimensions of how people learn from practice and help expand the knowledge base of teaching in the process.

LEARNING FROM PRACTICE AND RESEARCH

Our analysis of how teachers learn to lead joins the growing chorus of others working to show how teachers and researchers can collaborate to deepen our knowledge about teaching, learning, and leadership. We have made an effort to build knowledge from both academic research and teacher knowledge—thus enriching both. We show both the general and the particular, the conceptual and the practical, the universal and the local, the theory of researchers and the theory of those who practice. Each in its own way contributes to the knowledge of how teachers learn to lead. Our work is only a beginning, but we think it constitutes an important step in the right direction: in creating the conditions for collaboration between teachers and researchers, in building on teacher knowledge, and in finding a place where both academic knowledge and teacher knowledge enhance a deeper understanding of how teachers learn to lead.

The Vignette Authors:
Writing Project Teacher-Consultants

Local Writing Project site directors, as well as leaders from NWP's nationally sponsored programs, observe Writing Project teacher-leaders at work in a variety of settings. Therefore, we called on them to nominate 31 teachers who had successfully taken on leadership positions in their schools, districts, or states, or in NWP. We invited each NWP leader to nominate one individual whom he or she knew had the following characteristics:

- was professionally active;
- was reflective about work he or she had done to influence students, peers, and the contexts in which he or she worked; and
- was comfortable writing about this work.

Half the group was asked to recommend someone who played one or more leadership roles in the Writing Project and the other half was asked to recommend an individual who took leadership in other educational arenas (e.g., school, district, state). We accepted all nominated individuals.

During the project, we collected a professional history survey from the vignette authors. Of the vignette authors, 88% are women and 12% are men; 79% are Caucasian, 15% are African American, 3% are Asian American, and 3% are "Other." They come from 21 states and 31 Writing Project sites. Their leadership work spans all school levels: elementary, middle, senior high, and university. They participated in the Writing Project's Summer Invitational Institute between 1983 and 2004. On average, they had worked in education for 18.5 years. At the time of the study, 91% worked in education, while 9% were retired but continuing to work in education. In their last reported positions, the vignette authors were

- teaching (15/38.5%);
- working in school systems in positions such as assistant principal, curriculum specialist, or superintendent (11/28.2%); and
- working in education in positions such as curriculum specialist in state departments of education or consultant for their Writing Project sites (13/33.3%).

Table 1 highlights the characteristics of the 14 vignette authors whose full vignettes are included in this book.

Table 1. Characteristics of Featured Vignette Authors

Name	Chapter	Highlighted Leadership Roles	School Level	Gender	Race	Location	State
Anne H. Aliverti	Four	New-teacher mentor	Middle, High	Female	Caucasian	Urban	Washington
Elizabeth A. Davis	One	Teacher-leader	Middle	Female	African American	Urban	District of Columbia
Mimi Dyer	Three	Department chair	High	Female	Caucasian	Suburban	Georgia
Paul Epstein	Two	Reading specialist	Elementary	Male	Caucasian	Small city	West Virginia
Deidré R. Farmbry	Three	Principal, Regional superintendent	High, K–12	Female	African American	Urban	Pennsylvania
Shayne Goodrum	Four	District curriculum coordinator	Middle	Female	Caucasian	Urban	North Carolina
Christy James	Three	Master teacher	Middle	Female	Caucasian	Rural	South Carolina
Kim Larson	Two	State curriculum director	K–12	Female	Caucasian	N/A	Nebraska
Yarda Leflet	One	Assistant principal	High	Female	Caucasian	Suburban	Texas
Ronni Tobman Michelen	Two	Assistant principal	High	Female	Caucasian	Urban	New York
Scott Peterson	Four	District curriculum coordinator	Elementary	Male	Caucasian	Rural	Michigan
Austen Reilley	One	Teacher-leader	Middle	Female	Caucasian	Rural	Kentucky
Linda Tatman	One	Assistant director, Master of Arts in Teaching Program	University, Teacher Education	Female	Caucasian	N/A	Ohio
Lucy Ware	Four	District literacy coach, School-based literacy teacher	Elementary	Female	African American	Urban	Pennsylvania

References

Achinstein, B. (2002). Conflict amid community: The micropolitics of teacher collaboration. *Teachers College Record, 104*(3), 421–455.

Billmeyer, R. (2004). *Strategic reading in the content areas: Practical applications for creating a thinking environment.* Omaha, NE: Dayspring Printing.

Bransford, J. D., Brown, A. L., & Cocking, R. R. (1999). *How people learn: Brain, mind, experience, and school.* Washington, DC: National Academy Press.

Brown, J. S., & Duguid, P. (1996). Organizational learning and communities-of-practice: Toward a unified view of working, learning, and innovation. In M. D. Cohen & L. S. Sproull (Eds.), *Organizational learning* (pp. 58–82). Thousand Oaks, CA: Sage. [Reprinted from *Organization Science, 2*(1), Special Issue: Organizational learning: Papers in honor of (and by) James G. March (1991), 40–57.]

Browne-Ferringo, T. (2003, October). Becoming a principal: Role conception, initial socialization, role-identity transformation, purposeful engagement. *Educational Administration Quarterly, 39*(4), 468–503.

Cochran-Smith, M., & Lytle, S. L. (1993). *Inside/outside: Teacher research and knowledge.* New York: Teachers College Press.

Cochran-Smith, M., & Lytle, S. L. (1999). Relationships of knowledge and practice: Teacher learning in communities. *Review of Research in Education, 24,* 249–305.

Cochran-Smith, M., & Lytle, S. L. (2009). *Inquiry as stance: Practitioner research in the next generation.* New York: Teachers College Press.

Cohen, J. L. (2008). "That's not treating you as a professional": Teachers constructing complex professional identities through talk. *Teachers and Teaching: Theory and Practice, 14*(2), 79–93.

Coleman, P. T. (2006). Power and conflict. In M. Deutsch, P. T. Coleman, & E. C. Marcus (Eds.), *Handbook of conflict resolution: Theory and practice* (2nd ed.) (pp. 120–143). San Francisco: Jossey-Bass.

Collins, B. (1999). The first reader. In *Questions about angels* (p. 7). Pittsburgh, PA: University of Pittsburgh Press.

Crow, G. M., & Glascock, C. (1995). Socialization to a new conception of the principalship. *Journal of Educational Administration, 33*(1), 22–43.

Deutsch, M. (2006). Cooperation and competition. In M. Deutsch, P. T. Coleman, & E. C. Marcus (Eds.), *Handbook of conflict resolution: Theory and practice* (2nd ed.) (pp. 23–42). San Francisco: Jossey-Bass.

Deutsch, M., Coleman P. T., & Marcus, E. C. (Eds.). (2006). *Handbook of conflict resolution: Theory and practice* (2nd ed.). San Francisco: Jossey-Bass.

Dweck, C. S., & Ehrlinger, J. (2006). Implicit theories and conflict resolution. In M. Deutsch, P. T. Coleman, & E. C. Marcus (Eds.), *Handbook of conflict resolution: Theory and practice* (2nd ed.) (pp. 317–330). San Francisco: Jossey-Bass.

Freire, P., & Macedo, D. (1987). *Literacy: Reading the word and the world*. London: Routledge & Kegan Paul.

Friedrich, L., Lieberman, A., & Hall, S. (2009, April). *Revisiting the vignette as a qualitative method: Focusing on leadership learning*. Presented at the Annual Meeting of the American Educational Research Association, San Diego, CA.

Galindo, R., Aragon, M., & Underhill, R. (1996). The competence to act: Chicana teacher role identity in life and career narratives. *The Urban Review, 28*(4), 279–308.

Gawande, A. (2002). *Complications: A surgeon's notes on an imperfect science*. New York: Picador.

Gawande, A. (2007). *Better: A surgeon's notes on performance*. New York: Picador.

Gray, J. (2000). *Teachers at the center: A memoir of the early years of the National Writing Project*. Berkeley, CA: National Writing Project.

Grimmett, P. P., & MacKinnon, A. M. (1992). Craft knowledge and the education of teachers. *Review of Research in Education, 18*, 385–456.

Grossman, P., Wineburg, S., & Woolworth, S. (2001). Toward a theory of teacher community. *Teachers College Record, 103*(6), 942–1012.

Gutierrez, K. D., & Rogoff, B. (2003). Cultural ways of learning: Individual traits or repertoires of practice. *Educational Researcher, 32*(5), 19–25.

Hallett, T. (2007). The leadership struggle: The case of Costen elementary school. In J. P. Spillane & J. B. Diamond (Eds.), *Distributed leadership in practice* (pp. 85–105). New York: Teachers College Press.

Hargreaves, A. (2003). *Teaching in the knowledge society: Education in the age of insecurity*. New York: Teachers College Press.

Hargreaves, A. (2008). Leading professional learning communities: Moral choices amid murky realities. In A. M. Blankstein, P. D. Houston, & R. W. Cole (Eds.), *Sustaining professional learning communities* (pp. 175–197). Thousand Oaks, CA: Corwin Press.

Holland, D., Lachicotte, W., Jr., Skinner, D., & Cain, C. (1998). *Identity and agency in cultural worlds*. Cambridge, MA: Harvard University Press.

Holvino, E. (2001, June). *Complicating gender: The simultaneity of race, gender, and class in organization change(ing)*. (Working Paper No. 14). Boston: Center for Gender in Organizations, SIMMONS Graduate School of Management.

Hughes, L. (1994). April rain song. In L. Hughes, A. Ramersad (Ed.), & D. Roessel, (Ed.), *The collected poems of Langston Hughes*. New York: Alfred A. Knopf, Inc.

Ladson-Billings, G. (1994). *The dreamkeepers: Successful teachers of African American children*. San Francisco: Jossey-Bass.

Lave, J., & Wenger, E. (1991). *Situated learning: Legitimate peripheral participation*. New York: Cambridge University Press.

Lee, V. E., & Smith, J. (1996). Collective responsibility for learning and its effects on gains in achievement for early secondary students. *American Journal of Education, 104*(2), 103–147.

Lieberman, A. (1987). *Documenting professional practice: The vignette as a qualitative tool.* Paper presented at the Annual Meeting of the American Educational Research Association, Washington, D.C.

Lieberman, A. (2007). Professional learning communities: A reflection. In L. Stoll, & K. S. Louis (Eds.), *Professional learning communities: Divergence, depth and dilemmas* (pp. 199–203). Berkshire, England: Open University Press.

Lieberman, A., & Miller, L. (2004). *Teacher leadership.* San Francisco: Jossey-Bass.

Lieberman, A., Saxl E., & Miles, M.B. (1988). Teacher leadership: Ideology and practice. In A. Lieberman (Ed.), *Building a professional culture in schools* (pp. 148–166). New York: Teachers College Press.

Lieberman, A., & Wood, D. R. (2003). *Inside the National Writing Project: Connecting network learning and classroom teaching.* New York: Teachers College Press.

Little, J. W. (1982). Norms of collegiality and experimentation: Workplace conditions of school success. *American Educational Research Journal, 19*(3), 325–340.

Little, J. W. (1986). Seductive images and organizational realities. In A. Lieberman (Ed.), *Professional development in rethinking school improvement: research, craft and concept* (pp. 26–44). New York: Teachers College Press.

Little, J. W. (1995). Contested ground: The basis of teacher leadership in two restructuring high schools. *The Elementary School Journal, 96*(1), 47–63.

Lortie, D. C. (1975). *Schoolteacher: A sociological study.* Chicago: University of Chicago Press.

Mangin, M. M., & Stoelinga, S. R. (2008). *Effective teacher leadership: Using research to inform and reform.* New York: Teachers College Press.

McClelland, D. C. (1975). *Power: The inner experience.* New York: Irvington.

McDonald, J. P., Buchanan, J., & Sterling, R. (2004). The National Writing Project: Scaling up and scaling down. In T. K. Glennan Jr., S. J. Bodilly, J. Galegher, & K. A. Kerr (Eds.), *Expanding the reach of education reforms: Perspectives from leaders in the scale-up of educational interventions* (pp. 81–106). Santa Monica, CA: RAND.

McLaughlin, M. W., & Talbert, J. E. (2001). *Professional communities and the work of high school teaching.* Chicago: University of Chicago Press.

McLaughlin, M. W., & Talbert, J. E. (2006). *Building school-based teacher learning communities: Professional strategies to improve student achievement.* New York: Teachers College Press.

Miles, M. B. (1990). New methods for qualitative data collection and analysis: vignettes and pre-structured cases. *International Journal of Qualitative Studies in Education, 3*(1), 37–51.

Miles, M. B., Saxl, E. R., & Lieberman, A. (1988). What skills do educational "change agents" need? An empirical view. *Curriculum Inquiry, 18*(2), 157–193.

Morrison, T. (1973). *Sula.* New York: Alfred A. Knopf.

Morton, I. (1991). *Conflict resolution programs in schools.* ERIC/CUE Digest, Number 74. Columbia University, Teachers College, ERIC Clearinghouse on Urban Education New York.

National Writing Project, & Nagin, C. (2003). *Because writing matters: Improving student writing in our schools*. San Francisco: Jossey-Bass.

Nebraska Writing Project belief statements. (n.d.). Retrieved December 14, 2009, from http://www.unl.edu/newp/about/index.shtml

Nelson, B. S., & Sassi, A. (2005). *The effective principal: Instructional leadership for high-quality learning*. New York: Teachers College Press.

Normore, A. H. (2004, April). Socializing school administrators to meet leadership challenges that doom all but the most heroic and talented leaders to failure. *International Journal of Leadership in Education, 7*(2), 107–125.

O'Brien, T. (1998). *The things they carried: A work of fiction*. New York: Broadway Books.

Picasso, P. (n.d.) *Pablo Picasso quotes*. Retrieved March 8, 2010, from http://www.quotes.net/quote/3661

Ronkowski, S., & Iannaccone, L. (1989). Socialization research in administration, graduate schools and other professions: The heuristic power of Van Gennep and Becker models. Paper presented at the Annual Meeting of the American Educational Research Association, San Francisco.

Rossetti, C. (2001). Oh wind, where have you been? and Oh wind, why do you never rest? In C. Rossetti, & R. W. Crump (Ed.). *The complete poems* (pp. 230 & 232). London: Penguin.

Schön, D. (1983). *The reflective practitioner: How professionals think in action*. New York: Basic Books.

Sergiovanni, T. (2004). *Strengthening the heartbeat: Leading and learning together in schools*. San Francisco: Jossey-Bass.

Shulman, L. S. (1986). Those who understand: Knowledge growth in teaching. *Educational Researcher, 15*(2), 4–14.

Smith, K. (2006, December). Returning to the roots of true teacher leadership. In *Study of teacher-consultants and leadership: Vignettes* (pp. 237–243). Berkeley, CA: National Writing Project.

Smylie, M. A., & Denny, J. W. (1990). Teacher leadership: Tensions and ambiguities in organizational perspective. *Educational Administration Quarterly, 26*(3), 235–259.

Spillane, J. (2006). *Distributed leadership*. San Francisco: Jossey-Bass.

Spillane, J. P., & Diamond, J. B. (Eds.). (2007). *Distributed leadership in practice*. New York: Teachers College Press.

Stein, M. K., & Nelson, B. S. (2003). Leadership content knowledge. *Educational Evaluation and Policy Analysis, 25*(4), 423–448.

Stokes. L. (2005, August). *Taking on the real struggles of teaching: A study of the National Writing Project as an infrastructure for building practitioner knowledge*. Report to the MacArthur Foundation Network on Teaching and Learning. Chicago, IL: John D. and Catherine T. MacArthur Foundation.

Stokes, L. (2010). The National Writing Project: Anatomy of an improvement infrastructure. In C. E. Coburn, & M. K. Stein (Eds.), *Research and practice in education: Building alliances, bridging the divide*. New York: Rowman & Littlefield Publishing Group.

Stoll, L., & Louis, K. S. (Eds.). (2007). *Professional learning communities: Divergence, depth and dilemmas*. Berkshire, England: Open University Press.

Tatum, B. D. (1997). *"Why are all the black kids sitting together in the cafeteria?" A psychologist explains the development of racial identity.* New York: Basic Books.

Vygotsky, L. S. (1978). *Mind in society: The development of higher psychological processes.* Cambridge, MA: Harvard University Press.

Wenger, E. (1998). *Communities of practice: Learning, meaning, and identity.* New York: Cambridge University Press.

Whitman, W. (2006). O me! O life! In *Leaves of grass* (p. 305). New York: Simon & Schuster. (Original work published 1900)

Whitney, A. E. (2008). Teacher transformation in the National Writing Project. *Research in the Teaching of English, 43*(2), 144–187.

Wijeyesinghe, C. L., & Jackson III, B. W. (Eds.) (2001). *New perspectives on racial identity development: A theoretical and practical anthology.* New York: New York University Press.

Wing, L., & Rifkin, J. (2001). Racial identity development and the mediation of conflicts. In C. L. Wijeyesinghe & B. W. Jackson III, (Eds.), *New perspectives on racial identity development: A theoretical and practical anthology* (pp. 182–208). New York: New York University Press.

York-Barr, J., & Duke, K. (2004). What do we know about teacher leadership? Findings from two decades of scholarship. *Review of Educational Research, 74*(3), 225–316.

Zeichner, K. (1995). Beyond the divide of teacher research and academic research. *Teachers and Teaching: Theory and Practice, 1*(2), 153–171.

About the Authors and Contributors

Ann Lieberman is an emeritus professor from Teachers College, Columbia University. She was at the Carnegie Foundation for the Advancement of Teaching for a decade and has consulted and spoken all over the world on teacher development and leadership, networks and school-university partnerships, and educational change. She is now at Stanford University.

Linda D. Friedrich served as a senior research associate at the National Writing Project. She has worked in education reform and research for 2 decades. She studies teacher leadership, professional development, and professional community. She is now Director of Research and Evaluation at NWP.

Anne H. Aliverti currently teaches sixth-grade language arts and social studies at Eckstein Middle School in Seattle, Washington. In her 13 years with Seattle Public Schools, she has taught students and mentored teachers new to the profession for the Staff Training, Assistance, and Review Program.

Elizabeth A. Davis, a computer-aided design teacher at Phelps Architecture, Construction and Engineering High School in Washington, D.C., is a member of the advisory panel to the National Commission on Writing and the D.C. Area Writing Project. She is a contributing author to *Putting the Movement Back Into Civil Rights Teaching* and *Writing for a Change: The March on John Philip Sousa Middle School*.

Mimi Dyer, a National Board certified teacher, is currently the director of the Academy of Math, Science & Technology at Kennesaw Mountain High School in Kennesaw, Georgia. She has served in many capacities with the National Writing Project and the Kennesaw Mountain Writing Project, most recently as the codirector of Keeping and Creating American Communities. Publications include chapters in *Making American Literatures*, *Writing Our Communities*, and *Writing America: Classroom Literacy and Public Engagement*.

Paul Epstein has been codirector of the Central West Virginia Writing Project since its inception in 2003. He has served on the leadership team of the Rural Sites Network of National Writing Project, cochairing it from 2007 to the present. He has been teaching elementary school in Kanawha County, West Virginia, since 1987, most recently as an elementary reading specialist in Charleston, West Virginia. He is also a musician and songwriter with four CDs to his credit, including "School Bus Coming."

Deidré R. Farmbry is an educational consultant specializing in school improvement through collaborative inquiry and leadership coaching. She served the school district of Philadelphia for 28 years, with her career culminating as interim superintendent. She is the author of published speeches and essays, including "The Warrior, the Worrier and the Word." She was a member of the first group of teacher leaders of the Philadelphia Writing Project (PhilWP) and has participated in and supported PhilWP's activities for many years.

Shayne Goodrum is Team Lead for Comprehensive Needs Assessment for the North Carolina Department of Public Instruction. She has taught English, served on school improvement teams, developed curriculum, directed instructional coaching teams, and worked to support student achievement in many other roles at the school, district, and state levels. She is a fellow of the Capital Area Writing Project at North Carolina State University, from which she received her doctorate, and for which she consults in writing and adolescent literacy.

Christy James has taught middle school social studies and language arts in North and South Carolina for the past 13 years. She was codirector of a local Writing Project site, where she facilitated the Summer Institute and helped lead the annual Young Writers' Camp, and taught a course on writing children's books. She has made numerous presentations at literacy and social studies conferences and is a regular staff development presenter for local districts.

Kim Larson has been involved with the Nebraska Writing Project (NeWP) since 1995, facilitating several summer and school-year professional development institutes and participating in NeWP-funded study groups. She is currently an instructional facilitator with the Papillion–La Vista School District, where she supports the work of secondary teachers in curriculum development. Before this, she served as the reading and writing director with the Nebraska Department of Education, and taught first and second grade for many years in Lincoln, Nebraska.

Yarda Leflet is director of Academic Services at Hays Consolidated Independent School District (CISD) in Kyle, Texas. She has been in education for

14 years, serving as a middle and high school English language arts teacher, a reading specialist, an assistant principal, and an academic dean. She has been involved with the Central Texas Writing Project since 1999.

Ronni Tobman Michelen has taught English for over 20 years and is now a principal at a New York City high school. She was a teacher-consultant with the New York City Writing Project for most of her teaching life and has brought the Writing Project into her school to work with and support teachers. In addition, she was the co-president of the New York City Association of Assistant Principals and Supervisors of English for 2 years.

Scott Peterson recently retired after 34 years as a teacher and curriculum specialist for the Mattawan, Michigan, public schools. He is coauthor of the book, *Theme Explorations: A Voyage of Discovery*, and his articles have appeared in *The Quarterly*, *Breakthroughs*, *Plains Song Review*, *Michigan Reading Journal*, and other journals and anthologies. He currently works as an educational consultant and teaches writing classes at Western Michigan University.

Austen Reilley taught in a multiage intermediate classroom for 2 years in Ohio before teaching seventh-grade language arts for 7 years in Rowan County, Kentucky, where she started an after-school writers' group for girls. She has recently moved back to a fourth-grade position in the same district. She has filled various roles for the Morehead Writing Project since 2004, including directing advanced institutes in digital storytelling, serving as the site's technology liaison, and codirecting two summer institutes.

Linda Tatman taught at Lockland High School in Cincinnati, Ohio, through spring 2003. She is presently an assistant director of the Ohio Writing Project at Miami University in Oxford, Ohio, where she directs the project's Master of Arts in Teaching program and is responsible for evaluation of workshops. She has also facilitated the project's summer institute and has cotaught workshops on young adult literature, grammar and writing, and reading and writing strategies.

Lucy Ware currently teaches gifted and talented students at a Pittsburgh elementary school. Lucy served as a codirector of the Western Pennsylvania Writing Project (WPWP) for 8 years and has played an active role in it for 22 years. The National Writing Project published her piece "More Thoughts on Reading in the Summer Institute" in 2004. She is a past facilitator the National Writing Project Directors Retreat and facilitates the NWP Professional Writing Retreat.

Index